CONTEMPORIZING PRAGNYA
A Holistic Re-Vision

Edited by
Vatsal Naik
Gopa Guha

About the Authors

Dr. Bhaskar Vyas (1937) Plastic Surgeon and **Dr. Rajni Vyas** (1937) Obstetrician and Gynaecologist have contributed to their respective fields with research innovations. Dr. R. Vyas has made a seminal contribution to unexplained reproductive failure with a success rate of 55 per cent with her research protocol. This is highest success rate. Dr. B. Vyas' seminal contribution is to derive several products from stem cells obtained from fat. They have numerous research papers published. They have published over a score of books. Concept Publishing Company has published their books on the topic of philosophy, psychology and physics, viz. 'Contemporizing Raj Yoga', 'Experiments with Truth and Non-violence—China Challenged' 3rd Edition, 'Indian Handbook of Hypnotherapy' 4th Edition, Space Time Consciousness—Rationale of the Paranormal'. They are now working on a philosophical concept, 'Pragnya', to take it to an utilitarian application as 'Pragnya Quotient'. They finally introduced themselves as perennial students of philosophy.

CONTEMPORIZING PRAGNYA
A Holistic Re-Vision

Bhaskar Vyas
Rajni Vyas

CONCEPT PUBLISHING COMPANY PVT. LTD.
NEW DELHI - 110 059

ISBN: 978-93-5594-648-5 (HB)
ISBN: 978-93-5594-656-0 (PB)

First Published 2023

Published and Printed by

Concept
Since 1974

Concept Publishing Company Pvt. Ltd.
A/15-16, Commercial Block, Mohan Garden
New Delhi-110059 (India)
T: +91-11-41101460
E: publishing@conceptpub.com, *W*: www.conceptpub.com

Cataloging in Publication--Courtesy: D.K. Agencies (P) Ltd. <docinfo@dkagencies.com>

Vyas, Bhaskar, author.
Contemporizing pragnya : a holistic re-vision / Bhaskar Vyas, Rajni Vyas.
pages cm
Includes index.
ISBN 9789355946485 (HB)
ISBN 9789355946560 (PB)

1. Intellect. 2. Consciousness. 3. Neurosciences. 4. Cognitive science. I. Vyas, Rajni, author. II. Title.

LCC BF431.V93 2023 | DDC 153.9 23

Preview

'Contemporizing Pragnya: A Holistic Re-Vision' presents interesting examples from Indian writings to help the reader understand the complex nature of pragnya. The authors, Drs. Bhaskar and Rajni Vyas begin with a description of pragnya as our 'creative intellect', 'our discerning wisdom' and 'our perfect yet detached ability to understand', based in pure consciousness. This description continues with ease to the relevance of pragnya to live a healthy and happy life with the ultimate possibility of achieving perfect liberation or moksha through dissolution with Cosmic Consciousness.

The authors discuss how we can attain optimal functioning of this pure and intuitive intellect and also share an inspiring glimpse about further possibilities to realize the full potential of this Cosmic Intelligence or The North Star within, as the authors describe it so wonderfully.

Drs. Vyas are accomplished conventional medical professionals who describe themselves as 'philosophers in quest of understanding life and its various manifestations'. Drs. Vyas met in 1964 when were in their twenties. Their marriage allowed them to continue this quest while being active in their illustrious careers in medicine. In the 1970s, their quest led them to several institutions and renowned saints. They especially mention Rohit Mehta and Shridevi Mehta, theosophists living at Varanasi who made a profound impact on both of them. From then they have continued their quest with earnestness and with humility which belies their depth of knowledge and understanding.

In 'Contemporizing Pragnya: A Holistic Re-Vision' each reader gets a chance to explore their mental abilities delving far beyond the intellect, yet based in concepts drawn from science and medicine.

Dr. Shirley Telles
MBBS, PhD
(Neurophysiology)
Director,
Patanjali Research Foundation,
Haridwar, India

Preview

The book, "Contemporizing Pragnya: A Holistic Re-Vision" offers delightful enlightenment to its readers. The book's unique approach makes the reader travel through time from the days of Upanishads through the era of Mahatma Gandhi and Shri Aurobindo to the contemporary perspective of Dalai Lama, and Radha Bernier. The book deliberates on the undulations of the concept Pragnya from the integral perspective of oriental philosophy, as it presents the conceptualization in Vedas Vedanta, Buddhist philosophy, Zen philosophy. It critically analyses the cognitive, effective and behavioural components/ parameters of Pragnya by deliberating on its association with states of consciousness to quantum physics on one hand and with creativity and its intellectual expressions like Rabindranath Tagore's poetry, Ramanujam and Shakuntala Debi's mathematical wisdom, Stephen Hawking and Karl Popper insight on the other hand. The reader is intellectually elevated to a different level with the freshness of the authors' correlational analogy between Pragnya and brain behaviour, functioning of endocrine system (molecules of emotions), cognitive and social neuroscience. The story telling style and natural flow of the authors' description makes the book a gripping read. The book must be read by scholars of Indian philosophy and psychology, researchers in cognitive science and neuro-science discipline.

Dr. Urmi Nanda Biswas
Professor,
Department of Psychology,
The M.S. University of Baroda

Foreword

I have read through the pages of the summary you sent and I can say without any hesitation that the subject is very well introduced and I look forward to reading the subsequent.

You are evidently developing a subject of intuition. This intuition or Pragnya is a very strange thing. You cannot predict its arrival nor can you know when it arrives, you can be aware of it only after it goes, leaving behind its fragrance. I am sure you will deal with this all the time.

Rohit

Dated 18.6.1994

Rohit Mehta

Preface

प्रज्ञान ब्रह्म

Rohit Mehta was a friend, philosopher and guide across the continents to numerous people. He was our mentor too. He moulded our mindsets without imposing and helped us in desolution of our ego. When he wrote the foreword at a first glance we were enthralled. We started developing the theme—Pragnya—as intuitive insight. This was some 27 years ago.

Halfway through the manuscript, reason prevailed over ecstasy. With our scientific background, we have progressed through logical thinking. The age of reason is hardly 300 years old. Yet, immense benefits that have accrued to mankind are a product of dissective, analytical, logical, didactic and divisive scientific process. On the other hand, there is no litmus test to wisdom. Rishis are said to have a voice from the sky and thus derived intuitive insight. That insight was valid, as assessed with a long century old endurance. An individual may be basking in a fool's paradise when he proudly exclaims that this is *my* hunch and I believe in myself. This can be disastrous. We decided to pause, ponder further, mull for nearly three decades, and ruminate for further digestion.

Rohit Mehta—Rohitbhai as we called him—was a liberal thinker. He himself has disagreed with Mahatma Gandhi a few times; though the bond of affection between the two is a history. When we are revising Pragnya from intuitive insight to a holistic revision, we are sure he would have been pleased; if he were to be around.

This holistic revision incorporates a full blossoming of a flower that is Pragnya. Holistic concept considers that each and every part is an integral whole. Thus the contents include prehistoric times, history, recent and remote, philosophical precepts, proven only with logical positivism, current scientific knowledge regarding the process of thinking and molecules that generate thought processes.

There is a high degree of specialization in various disciplines. Therefore, even an erudite and avid reader will be primarily reading to derive pleasure. A philosopher would be averse to discuss the blood chemistry of emotions and *vice versa*. Rather than enduring boredom, chapters that invoke resentment may conveniently be skipped over. Fragrance will surely prevail.

We have constantly tried to keep an intelligent reader in sharp focus. Academic motivations of the authors are to provide a gateway to the disciplines of psychology and philosophy. Gitanjali Roy has a novel Psychometry test for Pragnya. This will justify psychology to be a scientific pursuit since science has to be having a parameter of measurement. The concept is not a part of any such syllabus or textbook so far, even in India.

Present generation, in pursuit of excellence is over stretched with time. A single chapter may be read in less than an hour while waiting to board a flight. The complete book is concise enough to read over a long duration of flight. For most, we hope, the fragrance will pervade. If it persists and prevails, it will be of interest to rediscover numerous petals.

Research is the ultimate ulterior motive. The research aims at inventing ideas and their progression with various ramifications. One or more hypothesis may be formulated. Hypothesis must undergo further validation by peers and mentors. A convergence is then established that it is plausible that the hypothesis may indeed be true. This needs to be taken to concept validation done with only a few real life studies. After empirical evidence so generated is found favourable statistically as well, then only a further experimentation with normal human subjects will provide a valid justification to be taken universally. Our process for psychometric scale for Pragnya has begun.

Vatsal Naik rendered invaluable help with transcription and research. We acknowledge our gratitude to him. Concept Publishing Company, even in these difficult times, has accepted to publish. Ashokbhai Mittal has been a friend indeed.

Bhaskar Vyas
Rajni Vyas

Contents

1
Introduction

Mahatma Gandhi stirred up the conscience of the nation by marching from Ahmedabad to a village, Dandi, in 24 days. Wisdom of Mahatma Gandhi is still debated, whether he was a clever politician, a philosopher or saint? Probably he was all of these at different phases of his life. More than 90 years later, a virtual Dandi March was resurrected. The obvious motivation was to pay homage to the Mahatma. But, a politician has his Pragnya focused on the next election, a statesman is concerned for the welfare of the nation and a philosopher king—that happens only in the Aristotelian dreams—would not only think for the greatest good of the largest humanity, but also be concerned about the happenings in the outer space.

We studied some writings by Gandhiji as narrated in his autobiography. We wondered about the relevance of this little autobiographical story book. Several pristine qualities of a sage would have contributed to the survival of this book even after several decades. Every time we revisit the book, one factor clearly emerges. Bapu was involved in the affairs of Gujarat Sahitya Parishad too and had given a thought to the formulation of Gujarati dictionary as well. His diction was a true reflection of his personality. He wrote in short, straight sentences. He had derived inspiration from Tolstoy, Ruskin and studied *Bhagavad*

Gita several times, yet his messages were conveyed in brief.

This is how we find a reason to revisit the concept of *Pragnya. Pragnya* has been extolled as having a profound meaning. It is said that there is no correct translation in English or other languages. Several Indian philosophers have defined the concept as discriminative wisdom, intuitive insight, wisdom so as to have foresight etc.

Sanskrit has been the language of Indian civilization. Historical background has given the language an aura of reverence. It has elegance, eloquence and when recited in a group, it gathers effulgence. This should be applied to correctly interpret the meaning of the word *Pragnya*. Pragnya is a Sanskrit word. It is included in most Indian languages that have roots in Sanskrit. However, translations in vernacular languages are also cited as Pragnya. Multiplicity of the meanings may be due to archetypal heritage.

Present day generations of young people across various disciplines are more centered with technology and information is generally derived with computers. Information providers of several kinds have yet not included the word Pragnya into their dictionary. Let us clarify. Pragnya encompasses all of the above and still much more. Suffice it to say that it is a natural attribute to all human beings. Right after birth, a child gathers information about the surroundings and develops a conceptual view of mother, family, friends, society and so on. This storehouse of memories will reverberate with numerous synaptic connections in the brain. Speed to establish the connectivity and its veritable functions will determine intelligence and personality of the individual.

Bifurcation of the concept to scientific paradigm may be frowned upon by Pundits. Yet, philosophy is the mother to all disciplines. Facts with empirical evidence may logically contribute to a higher paradigm shift.

Taking a lesson from Mahatma Gandhi, it should be direct and short, and also should convey the full meaning. It must be devoid of subjective projection.

Thus, *Pragnya* is pristine pure to the innocence of a child. As life unfolds, innocence encounters various kinds of vicissitudes. The impacts may vary from profound to ridiculous. It may cause a jerk to the stability of *Pragnya* so that it may undergo undulation. This study will discuss various facets of such undulations as well.

As a surmise, it should be appropriate to assume that every human being, is naturally a just human being, however it may be poised as a giant superhuman personality. Himalayan blunders may also occur that may not only determine the future life of a single individual, but even the fate of continence.

The concept is further enlarged with additional parameters such as location of the situation to be examined and assessed as well as the time when mind is applied to determine resolution. Obviously, *Pragnya* undulates. Such undulations of *Pragnya* call for a Re-Vision. Our first study on the subject happened to be some 40 years ago. We found ourselves like Alice in Wonderland. We formulated a book as follows:

It was titled

The Subtle Way to Wisdom

1. Introduction to the concept of Pragnya:

- Happiness, the universal desire and perennial quest.
- The stress and strife are infrequent outcomes of this pursuit. Frustration, failure and depression are also not infrequent. Was the choice of the goal or the method of achievement faulty?
- Standard methods of selection.

(a) Deductive, logical, statistical, rational, scientific method or

(b) based on belief or intuition. Wisdom is the masterful management of the unforeseen. Cosmic intelligence, the North Star within.

- What is ***Pragnya?***

2. Mirror images and Color Fountains:

- How the sensory inputs generate perception.
- Fallacies in perception.
- Conditioned reflex.
- Emotions and feelings.
- How they color the concepts?
- Preconceived notions, prejudices and stereotype behavior.

3. The mysteries of Mind:

- A continuous recording of all events in their totality.
- At the conscious, subconscious and unconscious levels, how the coloring process of projection, denial, transference, substitution, sublimation, repression, neurosis and other defense mechanisms operate in overt and covert manner.
- Thoughts, a product of the brain, are different from the gastric juices, a product of the stomach.
- The cybernetics of thought processes.
- Zen koan as the impossible question.

4. A computer Scan:

- Rational logical processing leading to a dialectical choice, the option being yes/no. The mathematical binary process incapable of taking into account the profound variability of qualitative abstraction. Instead, the computer operator plays games with a sole criterion of winning.
- Manipulation between the operator and the computer causing jarring of the function and marring of the resultant data, vitiating the results.

- Singularity of approach, a possible solution on account of concentration.
- Lasting solution is to locate the master manipulator and eliminate him.

5. The master manipulator:

- Dichotomy in thinking and behavior, a common occurrence.
- Motivation.
- The observer-observed phenomenon.
- Existence of more than one/several ego states.
- Ego as the driving force.
- Is it possible to have an auto-pilot?

6. Gathering Dust the mirror reflects no light:

- Conditioned reflexes culminating into stereotype behavior.
- The living not only become goalless, but also soulless.
- The loss of fragrance.
- A catastrophic experience, an eye-opener.

7. Vanishing trick in twilight:

- The Fantasied world of one's own creation in contrast to the existence of objectivity without the presence of self.
- Is there a possibility to be an actor in the play and still be in the audience?
- Is it possible to get out of the auditorium and yet return at will to join the play as a better actor? If yes, how?

8. The fourth dimension:

- Turya, the fourth state of consciousness.
- In the twilight, experience of restful alertness.
- Experience of gentle passivity and disappearance of the craving for the driver's seat leading to choiceless awareness.
- The dawn of experiential knowledge.

- Is it a mirage? Is it a delusion?
- Recourse to scientific method.
- Repeatable and reproducible with quantifiable results.
- Difference between predictable events and happenings.

9. Thought: The floating particles:

- Psychobiology.
- Relaxation response in contrast to stress response.
- Three biochemical pathways to stress response.
- A structured, physical modality with capacity for alarm reaction as well as sustained response—Autonomic Nervous System: Ida and Pingala—Sympathetic and parasympathetic nervous systems.
- Endocrines as sustained non-structured release of molecules in the blood with long lasting effects.
- Pulsatile biological clock.
- Immune system releasing complex molecules with the blood releasing molecular biomechanical substances in response to thought processes. Endorphins. Neuropeptides.
- Action of 'suprathalamic stimuli' through any or all of the mentioned pathways.
- Molecular biological events, their mediation via chemoreceptors.
- cAMP [**cAMP** is an adenosine triphosphate (ATP) derivative and used for intracellular signal transduction]. Genes and the double helix. Possibility of permanent change through genetic manipulation.

10. Charts to the pathless land:

- Buddha's classic masterprint: Madhyama Pratipada diverting into over 80000 methods of meditation.
- Patanjali Yoga Sutra.
- Transcendental meditation with extensive analytical and scientific reports.

- Tibetan tantra: Meditative modalities on compassion, samata, vajra and maitri. Vipassyana, kayanupassya and chittanupassya.
- Four faces of Buddha—Amitabh, Avlokiteshwar, Ranmukteshwar.
- Kalachakra meditation. Zen. Satori. Kevalya Pad and Samadhi. Kundalini.

11. Experiential happening: A circuitous path to short distance:

- Is it acquisition, empowerment, endowment or a discovery of an attribute?
- Aurobindo's concept of overmind.
- Pratyahara in Raj-Yoga.
- Tatsuya pragnya pratishta.

12. Fragrance of the rains:

- Clarity of perception.
- Soundness of reason.
- Validity of concepts.
- Sharpness of intelligence.
- Love.
- Creativity and Beauty in performance.
- Sat chit ananda.
- The mountains and the Stars: Story of Zen Buddhism about the home-coming of the explorer.
- Story of Aswapati's wanderings and birth of Savitri.
- Life and the universe still a mystery; to care about.
- Arrival of the alone to alone through a pathless flight leaving charts behind.

With self-reflection, it was found that the diction was full of metaphors. It was pedantic. Motivation seemed to be about showcasing. There was no pulse reading of the prospective reader. With this limitation, we gave up the first draft.

Thus taking the concept to contemporary times, the quality of intelligence, wisdom, the process of enhancement and occurrence of its eclipse as well as maintaining an equipoise need to be elucidated. Brevity is essential in communication during the present century. Yet, parsimony of words may be so exercised that the meaning is not lost. This we shall do in later chapters.

Any work may be further perfected with revision, recapitulation, rewriting, reciting and so on. Revising after a long time, as we are doing here, we have called a holistic revision. Such an exercise has produced works that are perfected beyond perfection as well. We intend to present evidences from real life to prove the point. Present century is a pinnacle of scientific achievement.

Empirical Evidence for Revision

1. There was an elegant postulation that the universe began with a Big Bang. Present day physicists dared even to prove this by providing empirical evidence. After starting the work on creating a model for Big Bang that took several years, Large Hadron Collider was fired in 2013. A virtual universe did get created. It even validated a Boson particle that Satyen Bose had conceptualized with mathematical theory about a 100 years ago.
2. Leo Tolstoy wrote the classic '*War and Peace*' about 7 times. The novel still endures as readable.
3. D.T. Suzuki revised '*The Zen Doctrine of No-Mind*' soon after World War II. That made it consistent with contemporary times.
4. Shri Aurobindo Ghosh started writing the epic, '*Savitri*' while he was in Baroda around 1907. He finalized the script a few decades later at Pondicherry, only a few years before his demise in 1950.

2
Pragnya—Pristine, Pure and Pragmatically Perfect

It is difficult to find a precise, corresponding word for the Indian classical concept of *Pragnya*. It has been loosely translated as intellect, intuitive intellect, pure consciousness, discerning wisdom, intuitive insight, and so on. The word Pragnya is derived from a prefix, 'Pra' and verb 'gña'. The prefix translates as intense and 'gña' translates to 'know'. It will thus be more appropriate to be faithful to linguistics. Let Pragnya be understood as meaning to know with intensity, in depth.

So let us begin by elaborating on the concept. Having done so, we will then try to analyze the factors that can possibly create a clouding of Pragnya. Finally, we shall attempt to describe how to attain and retain the clarity of Pragnya whereby one not only can lead a healthy and a happy life, but also may have a peaceful death without the possibility of rebirth. As per classical Indian tradition, this life is continued further with a rebirth. Only very very few can aspire to a state of dissolution in cosmic consciousness that is 'Moksha' as per Hindu tradition and 'Nirvana' as per Buddhism.

Let us see at the onset as to how does a computer decipher the data. It is elementary to say that it does so through programming.

This would mean that a letter of the alphabet, say "p" will be read as "p" as long as it is written according to a standard pattern fed into the computer through software. Given the slightest deviation, the computer will fail to recognize the letter as "p". With further advancement in technology, computers provide a few limited alternatives. This element is also unique to the human brain. On the same pattern, the brain can function to arrive at an understanding of certain facts which are not directly conveyed. Just as a computer throws out possible variations to a written letter or word incorporated into the program, brain also has a faculty to recall all that has been previously known. Though a computer program may be designed taking a cue from brain functioning, brain functionality goes beyond computers. It has the capacity to evolve newer ideas and concepts previously unknown with semantical synthesis of previous knowledge.

Semantics will scan the various different modalities of meaning. Some of them may be eliminated and a few may be retained to combine together as a synthesis. Thereby a new inference is arrived at.

We are all familiar with the sense of gut feelings, or a hunch or a flash of intuition. We are also told numerous stories of scientific inventions, occurring through a flash of intuition. Archimedes was suddenly bestowed with it and shouted, "Eureka!". Kekule deciphered the structure of benzene ring through a dream of six serpents. Each one of them was holding the tail of previous one by their mouth. That provided a clue to Kekule that benzene ring may be a hexagon. The experience of the intense creativity is described by Einstein. He described it as a rather vague play with the certain signs and more or less clear images that he called symbols. Such creative inventions do require a clear functioning of Pragnya. However, only a few are bestowed with such a creative faculty.

Creativity is a prerogative of very very few people—may be less than 1 per cent of total humanity. We shall discuss creative process later.

All creative processes, whether a scientific discovery or writing a poetry or painting a landscape are done with an execution that requires an altogether different state of consciousness. However, Pragnya is not the exclusive privilege of the geniuses, literate, or creative people only. It is a naturally occurring endowment from nature. It is the fundamental attribute of each and every human being, regardless of education or intellectual ability.

The discriminating wisdom may manifest in the form of incisive insight which may pierce through heaps of information so that a crystal clear idea or concept is materialized. Through the subtle push of Pragnya, the wheels rotating in the quagmire of confusing and contradictory facts gently find the motion again. The resolution of the paradox poised by the Zen master defying all norms of logic is through that pristine quality of brain. Several alternatives would have been available to find a resolution for an apparent paradox. Zen master weeds out all that is futile and insignificant and arrives at the execution with an expression. That not only satisfies a Zen master but also enlightens everyone with delight.

The concept of Pragnya is unitary, as in a single human being as well as it is collective. It is clearly evident in history and has been called as collective consciousness as well as guiding forces of history. The operations of the collective consciousness are evident in the revolutionary historical processes like Voting in India in 1977, or the upheavals in the communist world.

The concept is discussed in detail later. We think the concept is already enlarged further. Therefore, it is necessary to clarify a little further. So, at the risk of clarity we restate the fundamental Vedantic concept.

Vedanta postulated a unitary consciousness—referred to as Brahman. That was primordial. Before the beginning of the universe there existed a singularity that is referred to as 'Brahman'. When the singularity wanted to manifest in various forms, entire universe came into being; be it stars including sun that is the forefather of planets around it, galaxies and even the empty space that is a mother state of all particulate matter in the universe. Mother Earth acquired environment so as to create life on itself. The life has artificial, botanical and zoological boundaries, yet, at the onset it was one with the materials that constituted Mother Earth. Therefore, we all belong to Mother Earth and so we all are one at the source. However, human consciousness is unique. Probably there is no another consciousness of its kind in the entire universe; not discovered with intense probing also. Though it may be thus a singularity, it is naturally bestowed on all of us. Through apparent fragmentation, we all manifest ourselves as different beings so accepting that we limit our discussions only to the life on earth and further to human life, it entails that we are only artificially fragmented but at source are unitary.

Long before western psychology came to be defined as a discipline, the concepts were well articulated by Indian philosophers. Philosophy is the mother of all disciplines and not before a long time even western thinkers were putting philosophy and psychology together as one.

The precepts in Indian tradition are: Some of the organs function in such a way that we can perform physical work. These are termed as organs of work. We shall take this discussion later but focusing on psychic function at a thinking level there are psychic faculties which makes possible the functioning of our brain. These psychic faculties function at four levels. They are mana, chitta, buddhi, and ahankar. (The concept is not similar to the Freudian one of super ego, ego and id, nor it has connections with the theories of conscious and unconscious mind.) Taken all together, they contribute to what is described as Antahkaran, i.e. the inner faculty.

All the thought processes that occur in the brain either in sleep or in the waking state, conscious or the unconscious, deductive or intuitive occur through the functioning at these four planes. We shall therefore now attempt a brief elucidation of their meaning.

The Mana can literally be translated as the mind. The dialectic thought processes in the mind think in the pair of opposites. It is in the form of either this or that.

The chitta is that plane where there is a resolution of duality and its storage as a memory that may be recalled at will or it may go deep down into a plane that may be called unconscious mind. However, retaining the choice and executing it with endeavor and pursuit are the functions of the buddhi—intellect. Several qualities are ascribed to buddhi. The perimeter of intellectuation pervades far and wide. It has access to what is already learnt and stored in mana and chitta. Additionally intellectual processes so extend as to convert what is perceived as new into concepts. Further exploration by intellectuation may provide newer theorems and innovative meanings as well. It further guides execution of a resolution.

Ahankar is literally translated as the ego but it would be a misconception to equate it with the Freudian concept of ego. The modern psychology considers ego as the psychic self which constantly interacts with the super ego and id so as to maintain psychic equilibrium. The relevance of modern psychology is obvious. Though formulated less than 150 years ago, the discipline has prevailed across the universities in the world. Modern psychotherapy also is founded on these precepts.

Therefore, there is no need to deny this psychological framework.

However, modern psychology also has almost ignored the concept of Pragnya. It can be better understood with relevance to Indian format. Here the concept of 'Ahankar' is entirely alien to western concepts. So let us dwell at length on Ahankar. It takes us to the very beginning of the physical self and its roots into cosmic consciousness. This verges on mysticism. Therefore, we take recourse to *Mundaka Upanishad* where the concept is illustrated with a parable.

> "Two birds, united always and known by the same name closely cling to the same tree. One of them eats (I, the doer) the sweet fruit, the other looks on (I, the seer)."

I, the doer, is present in almost all human beings since we all do exist with our action. Yet, there is a transcendental, cosmic aspect to our existence that not only watches what is being done but also the entire tree on which the two birds are described as perched on. Rabindranath Tagore takes recourse to poetry to illustrate.

> "Two birds, beautiful of wings, close companions, cling to one common tree: of the two one eats the sweet fruit of the tree, the other eats not but watches his fellow. The soul is the bird that sits immersed on the common tree; but because he is not lord he is bewildered and has sorrow. But when he sees that other who is the Lord and the beloved, he knows that all is His greatness and his sorrow passes away from him. When, a seer, he sees the Golden-hued, the maker, the Lord, the Spirit who is the source of Brahman, then he becomes the knower and shake from his wings sin and virtue; pure of all stain he reaches the supreme identity."

Poetic visions summarise with lot of parsimony, but this poetry also has used words and phrases like Lord, the maker and the Spirit, they go into abstract, obscure and occult realm. Who are we to edit or criticize a Nobel Laureate for is prize winning poetry? Poetic visions extend far beyond the dictionary meaning of the words. Moreover, scientific meanings to the esoteric words like Lord etc. are beyond reasoning. A long dialogue with the poet as to what he meant by dedicating his poetry—*Gitanjali* to the Lord may attract a thesis at Vishwabharati University. We restrict ourselves to what is pertinent to Pragnya discussion. Let us further rationalize.

The two birds are in fact so united that they are known by the same name, stay together always, perch on the same tree. It is a simultaneous existence of the two. The two birds are existing at the same spot and at the same time, yet they are distinctly different when performing their activities. They perform different action. One eats the fruit of the tree, may also jump to and fro, dance with delight and express sorrow if the fruit turns out to be unpleasant. The other sits still and looks on.

Let us not lose the sight of the fact that basically, at their roots, intrinsically in a psychic sense, two birds are coexistent. There is a witnessing in the midst of participation. When with little self-reflection, we realize that almost everyone has the experience with introspection so as to audit, edit, modify, justify etc. Herein the mystery of two birds dissolves.

The witnessing is not after the action of eating is completed by the first bird. The eating and the witnessing are simultaneous. Here we see what self explicit is and what is derived with introspection. With the same corollary, it can be extended further that physical existence is being witnessed by cosmic consciousness.

Herein lies the importance that Indian psychology will incorporate Pragnya as well. Pragnya also includes as to what I, the doer bird will select to eat, to execute, to perform with persistence and what not to eat as well. The choice will be determined by the personality of the person. Personality will be ingrained with three *gunas,* namely, *Satva, Rajas* and *Tamas.*

While Ahankar in the Vedic sense should be translated as 'I-ness or feeling of a distinctive individual self'. It may be clearly appreciated that the roles ascribed to ego and superego by modern psychology are functions at the level of Mana, Chitta, and Buddhi. The I-ness has two components: I, the doer and I, the seer. It is a common experience for all of us to say that I am watching myself as to how I am doing a particular thing. This distinction has relevance when we will discuss about sustaining the clarity of Pragnya while engaged in the activity.

Seeing oneself as an executor of an action is that I—Ahankar as I, the doer. Outward expressions of all the actions as performed are performed by I, the doer. Motivation for action arises out of numerous necessities for sustaining life. A step beyond in motivation is performance of one's duty, regardless of mundane necessities.

I, the seer, is also incorporated in personal self. But, the form is a transcendental consciousness. Indian tradition is firmly rooted in the concept of a soul. The soul at its beginning was one with Consciousness that was the first to evolve. Say, at Big Bang, when universe arose, the first creation was Consciousness. Let us call this as primordial cosmic intelligence. The need and motivation for cosmic consciousness was simple, just to be. To be and to manifest without seeking any gratification whatsoever. It exists in its own right.

So, let us understand what the 'gunas' mean and how do they affect personality. The Vedanta postulates that out of absolute reality which is eternal, formless and eminent, the universe came into being through an interaction with Maya or Prakriti. The initial form arising out of the three qualities: Sattva, Rajas and Tamas. The rajasic element manifests as activity and is causative process of all creative processes. The Tamasic factor is responsible for the stability and rest. The Sattva maintains the harmony.

The three gunas balance the activity of each other and their orchestrated functioning results in clarity of Pragnya and soundness of the body, commonly said as a healthy mind within a healthy body. The balance between the three gunas can be disturbed.

The preponderance of sattva can bring about an exaggerated use of self-satisfaction, self-glorification, and going to the sense of self-indulgence. It may further lead to division of the other two. The excess of rajas leads to incessant activity, finally leading to a maniacal state of obsessive compulsion to work. We have coined the word 'workaholics' for the same. Excess of tamas causes oversleeping, inactivity and depression.

There could be a paradoxical state also; like a heart full of compassion and mind so full of sorrow that its faculties are blunted. If at all the mind functions, it ponders over the imponderable. In the process, even when the speech and the thought processes appear to be wise on the surface, they are hollow and stuff less. One is given to brood over the past knowing full well that it cannot be mended. There is a state of conflict between the impulses derived from the senses and the interpretation that the mind desires to give them. The unsteadiness arising of such a projection leads one astray. This is an account of wondering over endless number of alternatives. In desperation, such a person tries to aim at the end result. Such an achievement with such a state of mind is obviously impossible. This enhances the feeling of smallness and helplessness. Even if one were to take recourse to the classical texts, aiming only at the end results it would cause a delusion. Such a recourse adds to the confusion.

The process of the delusion begins by constantly dwelling on the objects of the sense. Persistent pursuit of such objects causes attachment, desire and subsequent craving for them. This can cause jealousy, competition and false perception. Projection arising out of the delusion leads to impaired memory. This in turn affects the functioning of mana, chitta and buddhi.

However the process is not irreversible. There is a definite way out, with well laid out steps to retrieve the brilliance of one's intellect. If the self-correcting psychocybernetics were to prevail, there may be a restoration to normalcy. This is known to occur in several human situations time and again, may be with repose, good counseling by friends and family, and at times by seeking the advice of the mentors.

But before we go on to that discussion, we add.

> Most of the times introspection may be sufficient, even when a giant blunder may have been committed. Let us illustrate with empirical evidence derived from Mahatma Gandhi.

He launched the Civil Disobedience Movement by announcing at a meeting at Ahmadabad in 1920. But he writes:

> "Almost immediately after the Ahmadabad meeting I went to Nadiad. It was here that I first used the expression 'Himalayan miscalculation' which obtained such a wide currency afterwards. Even at Ahmadabad I had begun to have a dim perception of my mistake. But when I reached Nadiad and saw the actual state of things there and heard reports about a large number of people from Kheda district having been arrested, it suddenly dawned upon me that I had committed a grave error in calling upon the people in the Kheda district and elsewhere to launch upon civil disobedience prematurely, as it now seemed to me. I was addressing a public meeting. My confession brought down upon me no small amount of ridicule. But I have never regretted having made that confession. For I have always held that it is only when one sees one's own mistakes with a convex lens, and does just the reverse in the case of others, that one is able to arrive at a just relative estimate of the two."

The last two sentences written by Bapu long long time ago, tantamount to sound psychological strategy so as to keep one's own vision clear. While taking a re-Vision, important advice to remember is not to add any guilt feeling.

It is pertinent here to describe the qualities of clear Pragnya. An individual with illumined qualities is not burdened by the past. He has patience and understands the life processes. Such patience gives him the equanimity to accept happiness or grief without being disturbed. While accepting the happiness and the sorrow, he is aware that the emotions caused by them may be fleeting impressions. Such an awareness arises out of an understanding that the unreal does not exist, while the real can never cease to be. When such a faith is built up, it follows that one can keep on doing what is the duty ordained at a given time with equipoise and without being bothered about the end result: be it happiness or grief, gain or loss, victory or defeat. The intelligence in this state is communion with the universal consciousness, i.e. to act according to the rules of Nature. Therefore, it directs the action in such a way that it does not leave its after-effects. On the contrary, the singularity leads to a resolute intellect. A resolute intellect is devoid of duality and it is firmly established in purity and is not possessed by the possession. He is truly possessed of his self and therefore can be said to be truly wealthy. A wealthy person need not be concerned about the routine transactions. Similarly, a person in communion with the cosmic consciousness—a yogi is involved in action without attachment. In such a state, gain and loss that is a part of mundane worldly affairs, disappears.

With this kind of enlightened intelligence, the inward reconciliation and the outward participation go on simultaneously in harmony. Individual then takes refuge in pure intelligence which is inspired by Nature. The actions performed in such a state not only become perfect but are devoid of any reaction. The mind is totally mastered and ruled by the intellect. The didactical discussion disappears. Consequently, the desires die out. He is satisfied to be himself. In this state of illumined intellect, he is neither overjoyed, nor is he downcast by the happenings around him.

Since the mind has acquired a state of serenity, all his sense organs now wither away from the cravings for satisfaction. He becomes truly dedicated to what is ordained as a right action with right perception. If one were to stand resolute, in such a state, there will be no regret and no guilt.

Clouding of Pragnya may indeed be perceptible as likely to occur with certain premonitory signs.

At a materialistic level, the sense organs decipher pleasure and pain. It might be considered elementary that the mind shall pursue pleasurable objects and shun the painful ones. However, without going into the depths of any philosophy, it is elementary to perceive that not all painful processes lead to unhappiness. While a sheer pursuit of pleasure can be catastrophic. Except for some rare exceptions like that of Charvaka, the materialistic philosophy based on pleasure principle does not find ground in Indian philosophical tradition. Instead, it dwells primarily on the fragility, futility and fragmentation of the fruits derived through the functioning of the sense objects. It is in this context that Shankaracharya proclaimed 'the world is unreal'.

Judging the ultimate outcome of senseless spending today as bankruptcy for times to come, the mind can decipher pleasurable expense of today as a painful experience and *vice versa*. Therefore, the mind is indeed a sixth sense organ. This is because of its faculty to superimpose the sensory perceptions with a meaning of its own.

However, for the uninitiated, the mind is likely to pursue the pleasures derived from the satisfaction of the senses. This will then lead to dwelling of the mind on the objects of pleasure. It then becomes a conditioned reflex and causes attachment to these objects. In the Pavlovian model, the dog's mouth starts watering at the ringing of the bell, even though the food is not around. This will inflame the desire when not fulfilled, the frustration can cause anger. In such a state, the perception gets deluded. There is no scope now for balancing the choice or executing the choice perfectly: leave aside any intuitive illumination of the whole process.

Before we discuss the methodology of keeping the Pragnya clear, it is pertinent to elucidate as to how a person should be guided to act if he is not to be driven by his senses. In the classical tradition, there is a ceremonial ritual called "yagna". This can be an elaborate ritual. It is designed as an offering. Quite often the meaning is lost in the performance of the rituals. It would then be a waste of precious food material. When viewed in its true meaning, it offers the fruits of actions to the divine. There are several ways by which I, the doer can be removed from the drama of the action.

One of the ways is to assume the role of I, the seer, whereby it will be naturally easy to offer all the consequences of action to the divine. Since the consequences are no more under my control, they do not bind me. In this way the chain of Karmic connection is disconnected.

If it were not possible to remove, I the doer, from the stage, like the director, one can take on the role of being an instrument through which all actions are done. There is yet another way. Even while acting with the sense of I, the doer, the actions are so selected as to cause the largest benefit to the largest number of people. Such actions invite leadership qualities and the end result of them are good because many would emulate the actions of the leader. In the process, it is likely to happen that the person so acting would realize the smallness of acting with an aim to get the reward from the actions. When so enlightened, the leader can harness the energies of the uninitiated ones without unduly disturbing them. A few leaders are indeed born as leaders. Most of them have discovered themselves to be much larger than life when they have seen large following at their rallies. What a halo effect would that produce!

One who has given up the desire to act for the fruits of the actions finds it easy to remain ever satisfied. He is therefore without desires. Therefore, he has not to decide to initiate any action for the satisfaction of his desires. This way he is automatically freed from the process that can cloud his Pragnya. Having thus offered all his actions to the divinity, he is free from the Karmic connections. In such a state, the Pragnya gets illuminated and the consciousness is pervaded by spirituality. For such a person, the actions natural to him are easily defined and he sees the goodness arising out of them. It is not likely therefore for him to be attached to or to seek alternative modalities of performance even though it may appear easy. Thus wastage of energy with dialectical analysis is conserved.

Performing action in any one of the above way can lead to a subtle psychological state. Such a doer while performing even his own inaction in the performance, may be a form of right action. This is best illustrated in the prudent behavior of an obstetrician. When conducting a delivery, his/her actions are not causing the birth of the baby. Physiological processes that cause the delivery of the baby are natural. The uterus contracts, the cervix dilates. This is spontaneous. He/she is waiting on the lady in labour, without interference; that inaction not to interfere is the right action.

Appreciating such a subtlety of the action and inaction, the intelligence gets focused in knowledge. All the doubts disappear in the light of such knowledge. Wisdom dawns. Such knowledge causes one to be freed from the overburdening oneself with responsibilities that the actions are capable of creating. Since there is freedom from the initiating action, this state is bondless. There is as well a lack of desire to keep on with the company of the process. It is further enhanced by detachment from the fruits of action. Such a philosophical disposition produces a state conducive of creating communion with the universal consciousness.

Shankaracharya derided action and extolled the merits of knowledge contending that only knowledge can illumine the intellect. This has been at times understood that he advocated that it is impossible for anyone not to be involved in action, since inaction can itself be a mode of acting. He has, therefore, explained the action as an object which by itself is devoid of any quality. It is the doer who imparts the merits and demerits to an action by the motivation. The motives of courage can be modulated through knowledge. It is, therefore, said that action performed by illumined intelligence accompanied through knowledge are not binding. It is wisely said that at times discretion not to act is better than to show off valor.

Since there is no overburdening with responsibility in such a state of action, the knowledgeable person is free from the garbage that goes along with faulty action. He neither desires nor does he envy. His very mode of action being that of dedication to the right action, keeps him untouched by the process of action.

Of course, any action would involve performance by the sense organs, the organs of action and the activity of mind and intellect. A wise person with steady intellect does perform such activity in his body as well as in the psyche but he is enlightened enough not to get entangled in that process.

The ancient Indian physician Charak expounding an all pervading hypothesis for health and illness, he said the faulty function of Pragnya is the cause of all mental illnesses. The Sanskrit word for good health is "Swastha". It means one who is steady in his self. It naturally follows that one who is not established in his steady Pragnya is likely to act on such a plane that he may cause a physical or psychical injury to himself or to others. Charak further explained that Pragnya consists of three components.

These three components are intellect, steadiness and forbearance, and memory. In view of the discussion regarding the modes and motivation of actions as we have seen, now any of these factors can lead a person to act in such a way that may cause ill health.

Such a pathogenesis is all encompassing to mental illnesses. It interesting to compare the modern methods of coping as the stress as discussed later (Chapter 7: Mind is like a mirror).

The Indian tradition does not stop at the wise counsel. It accepts the need to keep the Pragnya polished so that its purity is constantly maintained. This would be particularly true for the modern age. We have increased our memory contained and are constantly vying with each other to increase the speed at which it can be done. Therefore, it is not unusual to lose patience while racing against the time. This race can also endanger the steadiness of intellect.

The *Bhagavad Gita* and Patanjali's *Yoga Sutra* provided blueprint not only for maintaining the clarity of Pragnya but also for its penetration into subtler realms. After having acquired the understanding of the processes in the realm of the psyche and the involvement or the disengagement of the self therein, one has to be guided by an intense yearning for the inquiry into the ultimate reality. The results of the inquiry will begin with the first step itself. Such an inquiry would do away with the 'I- ness'. It would then generate a sense of dedication and devotion to the forces beyond ordinary comprehension. Having attained this state, one is able to undertake a way almost identical with the Madhyam Pratipada of Buddhism. The food habits and behavior as well as the protocol for action, sleep and even dreams do not deviate to any undue extremes. The chitta instead of making choices from the dialectics of mind is diverted to inquire into the inner realms of the self so that it is like a lamp which is without any quivering. Now, it is impossible to experience any contact with unhappiness or pain. This is what the classical Indian tradition calls as 'Sadhana'.

In the adversity the intellect is protected by boundless patience. In such a state of peace the rajas subsides and a realistic perception of permeation of universal consciousness in all the beings dawns. If the mind were to waver as its fundamental tendency, it has to be controlled through practice and detachment.

Thereafter Pragnya would undertake further journey into the subtler realms of what Shri Aurobindo calls as a "supermind and illuminated mind".

Patanjali not only provides the guidelines for opening the doors to and maintenance of Pragnya, it also, through eight-fold path opens the portals for journey into the subtler realms. It begins with four outward steps that dictate the behavior. It advocates non-violence, truthfulness, avoidance of stealing and indulgence and possessiveness. The second step advocates purity, contention, austerity, study of the self (introspection) and dedication to the higher power. Other steps are the practice of asanas and pranayam.

With the pratyahar, which means the withdrawal of mind from the sense objects, the journey within begins. The awakened Pragnya will hold on steadily to the path taking one face to face with the ultimate reality. The final step in the end of the journey may be called 'samadhi', a choiceless awareness, a communion with the divine consciousness, or the submergence into the ultimate reality. Such a prosaic elucidation of lofty philosophical concepts may appear to be high and dry to many a well inclined people. To them there is a simple, yet all encompassing key. This is to abandon all the dialectics and dedicate oneself to the divine with full faith.

The entire process of limitation of Pragnya in an individual and its subsequent journey into the subtler realm is symbolized in the epic by Shri Aurbindo, *Savitri*. It is full of beauty, lucidity and inspiration. The author has written some twenty four thousand lines. It is written in the style of the Upanishads where the supreme truths are symbolically conveyed through fables and parables. The author, therefore, calls it a legend and a symbol. Beginning with the character of a king who is the master of the horses, it describes the attributes of the mind and its horizontal journey through the plains of the world such as trade and commerce. However, his life is barren since he has no child. He qualifies for the blessings when he totally surrenders to the divine. He asks to be bestowed with Pragnya as follows:

> "Pack with eternal might one human hour and with one gesture change all future time. Let a great word be spoken from the heights. And one great act unlock the door of fate."

And a female child is born to him as Savitri. She is described as:

> "A lamp was lit, a sacred image made,
> A meditating ray has touched the earth
> Bridging the gulf between man's mind and God's
> Translating heaven into human shape.
> Its brightness linked our transience to the unknown."

The feminine consciousness denotes Pragnya. Let it not be understood that it is only a prerogative of female sex. There is a symbol of the Creator of universe as 'Ardhanarishwara'. Thus feminine consciousness is common to both the sexes. Pragnya alone, though an attribute of all, empowers a few to travel into higher realms of consciousness. We shall see the creativity as a process of invention later in (CH-5 Creativity, a Privilege of all).

The decisions concerning execution can be wise, mature, lasting and holistic only when the Pragnya is clear. While being a natural attribute, we have seen how it can be clouded due to stress, strain, motivation and indulgence in daily life. We shall see in the later chapters further facets concerning Pragnya in a holistic manner. Each chapter is written so as to provide a full picture that can as well be empirically illustrated with one line, such as, "A rose is a rose is a rose." or "Was it not said with a less mystic way by Shakespeare that, "A rose by any other name would smell just as sweet!"

Note

1. Mehta, Rohit (1970). *The Call of Upanishads*, New Delhi, pp. 139-141.

3
Pragnya since Antiquity to as of Now

The concept first occurs in the most ancient Vedas, the *Rig Veda* (1500-1000 BCE).[1] It translates literally as follows, 'that the radiant one, who feeds and nourishes, who ensures births, who desires association with the learned, he surely soon gains wide varied knowledge and becomes intelligent and aware.'

The concept is further expanded by the unknown Sage as, 'that those who constantly strive to understand the ways and methods of the objective world and its origin and its being surely attain divinity.'[2]

Rig Veda teaches thus: The quality of intelligence that is named as 'Pragnya' happens to be acquired by those who associate with learned, wise people. That increases intelligence so that the personality glows. Such persons relentlessly strive to understand the objective world as governed by Natural laws. *Rig Veda* has survived several thousand years. It is considered to be *Apurusheya* meaning thereby not spoken by human beings. Rishis heard the voice from heaven and transferred it to their disciples with memory. Yet, even before the civilization in India may have identified itself as Indus Valley Civilization, and thereafter Hindus translating that as Hindu civilization, this was probably the first treatise by any civilization. Hindu pantheon of gods has crores of deities. *Rig Veda* has not a single mention of any God. Thus the treatise should be considered as a heritage for the entire mankind.

Rig Veda discusses cosmogenesis as arising out of 5 basic elements. They are Agni, Prithvi, Jala, Vayu and Aakash; translated as Fire, Earth, Water, Air and Sky. Each of them has a distinct relationship with human intelligence. We confine ourselves to discuss as a summary what *Rig Veda* says about Pragnya. Wisdom there enunciated as Pragnya thus may be considered axiomatic.

We shall discuss contribution by Charak (600-500 BCE) in precedence to other texts that are likely to be antedated. This is being done since our present hypothesis concerning 'Pragnya' finds first ever eloquent definition and exploration in *Charak Samhita*. Charak was a rishi, philosopher who first translated the philosophical concept 'Pragnya', into utilitarian mode. He first defined what constitutes the psychic quality, Pragnya. He said it consists of 3 psychic elements, *Dhi, Dhruti* and *Smruti,* translated as intellect, persistence with patience and memory. Charak is the father of Ayurveda. The treatise is once again unique as being the first book on health, aetiology and pathogenesis of ailments and therapeutics mainly derived from herbs. Ayurveda has its genesis in Charak ascribing pathogenesis of all physical ailments to the dysfunction of Pragnya[3].

Modern medical science has identified numerous causative factors that contribute to aetiology of diseases. Charak's wisdom is indeed great but such a wide sweep to include *all* diseases arising from a fault in functioning of Pragnya seems to be rather far-fetched. *Charaksamhita* describes mainly psychosomatic conditions. Wisdom of Charak is still applicable when psychosomatic conditions are being discussed. For instance, depression is a psychic disorder. Its causes may be from the environment or are inbuilt genetically. During depression,

Pragnya, howsoever brilliant the individual may be, flows at a low ebb.

Charak succinctly explored several psychosomatic disorders that can be attributed to arise from faulty functioning of Pragnya. To name a few here:

1. Migraine connotes an unresolved conflict.
2. Irritable bowel syndrome connotes overwhelming sympathetic activity arising out of multitasking with rapid speed resulting in stress.
3. Phobia is an irrational fear arising out of faulty perception.

We shall discuss more about mental manipulations that progress to psychosomatic disorder later.

Shri Rama (700-400 BCE), during his adolescence, is said to have suffered from depression. Rishi Vashishtha was his mentor.[4] Counselling is voluminous. This is briefly described in Yajnavalkya. However, with this kind of psychotherapy, the eclipse of Pragnya of Rama was cleared. Authorship of *Yogavashishtha* is debatable between Valmiki and Vashishtha. It has no relevance here.

The treatise is narrated in Upanishad style storytelling. It elaborates on the power of thought so that every individual creates a world image—Leela. In this dance drama, each individual is a creator and actor as well. Interpolation by a subject with his own mind gives different colours to the world image. Every time the bottom line of the thought, then, emerges in favour of the self. This defaults the perception. False perception will lead to false action.

Adverse effects of false action may be catastrophic or may be such as to tend to be corrected with psychocybernetics. Intuitive insight may be a guiding torchlight. The end of the treatise leads to a pathway as to how to cultivate intuitive insight.

Rishi Patanjali elaborates on 7 states of consciousness. In each of these states, there is a presence of self-awareness that exists, except in the seventh. Most people are aware of the ordinary awareness state, sleep state, and dream state and are conscious of the fact that there is obvious self-awareness. The door to seven states of consciousness begins with a gateway to the fourth—Turya—state of consciousness[5]. The perception in the fourth state gets highly modulated. There is only a faint distinction between virtual and the real. It is described as 'tranquil settlement in the state of liberation and the state of witness in action'. Fifth, sixth and seventh states are highly esoteric. Apart from clarifying perception, achievement up to the seventh state generates the vision of ultimate reality. It is difficult to describe in words, but may be quoted as, 'that which has no parts, soundless, the incomprehensible, beyond all the senses, the cessation of all phenomena, all blissful and non-dual AUM. Seventh state culminates into *Samadhi*. In this state of *Samadhi,* the philosophical basis is based on the hypothesis that axiomatically the universe arose from a single point. May be called the Big Bang by modern physics. Rishi Vashishtha would call the beginning as AUM or Bramha. The derivation we aim at is to experience oneness with all that is in the cosmos. *Samadhi* thus achieves unity with cosmic consciousness. Here, there is absolute disappearance of the mind; that is the journey by one *alone* to That Alone. Boundaries such as space and time also disappear so that there is unity with cosmic consciousness.

Rishi Patanjali (200 BCE) has emphasised on the presence of Pragnya in any one of the above 7 states.[6] States of consciousness are distinctly different and well defined, yet, Pragnya pervades them all. Patanjali has also a short aphorism on flowering of Pragnya. How that happens as an exuberance of all the constituents of the personality profile of an individual has been dwelt upon.[7]

Another classical example is Arjuna (400 BCE). Mahabharata is said to be the motherground of all storytelling. *Bhagavad Gita* in *Mahabharata* is said to be the last Upanishad. The story goes that before the start of the war between cousins, the bravest warrior Arjuna was stricken with grief. He suffered thinking about the consequences of a war fought for material gains. But, his mentor Krishna explored the numerous psychological factors that could have clouded Arjuna's Pragnya. *Bhagavad Gita* has now become sacrosanct. It may also be described as an authentic text for psychotherapy. Krishna counsels while seated as a charioteer of 5 horses.[8] The horses connote a metaphor for the five senses. Pragnya undulations have to be so controlled as to generate a state where action is given a sure and certain direction. That will not veer away from right action. Even the personality profile of a person whose Pragnya is stable is described in detail such as his demeanour of sitting, walking etc.

'But those who are temperate in eating and recreation, balanced in work, and regulated in sleep, can mitigate all sorrows by keeping the mirror of their mind clear, free from dust.'[9] Stability of Pragnya is dependent upon appropriate nourishing food, dwelling in a healthy environment and working only with eustress as may be needed. Inference may as well be derived from spoken speech as well as body language.

Motivation gives the direction for action. Most of the motivations arise from cravings by the mind. A person who is satisfied by whatever merits he has achieved and acts so as to be propelled in action not by ulterior motives but in the larger interest of the largest number of people may aspire for stability. He has the courage to change the situation that is liable to change. He also understands the limitations of action that cannot change circumstances. He then accepts them gracefully. A man with stable intellect has the wisdom to differentiate between the two situations. Herein comes the role of Pragnya superseding the role of intellect and psychological memories and keeping all three gunas in balance.

Up and down modulation of Pragnya arises from manipulations by the mind. Sorrowful events as well as pleasuresome happenings are common vicissitudes in life. A person with the stability of Pragnya can easily walk out of grieving as well as revelling in pleasure.

Life means relationships. Every relationship will enjoin a reciprocal obligation. It should be fulfilled that far; and no longer. Most people come to a down gradation of intellectual faculties when their action is seen through a prism of attachment.

Narration concerning Pragnya in *Bhagavad Gita* is widespread. The entire discussion can itself be a large volume. What we have narrated would suffice for arriving at a mathematical formula for Pragnya quotient. That will be a generic ground for performance through a right choice for action. So, let us understand how powerful a thrust may be given with the power of thought.

After Antiquity, let us now Derive Inspiration from Modern History

One of the parameters regarding veracity of a statement is its reverberation from antiquity to modern times. Truth is only one, but, one of the parameters of a fact being true is the lasting value of a concept. Pragnya concepts as described in ancient texts are reverberated, maybe in different words in modern times as well. Since poets derive inspiration and recite the poems, they are best suited as empirical examples.

Sri Aurobindo poetically created a version of Savitri. The epic poem is a metaphor which is still recited by numerous devotees and tangible to a few is indeed a quest for the highest state of Pragnya. Savitri encounters 3 higher states of existence as Mother of Compassion, Mother of Power, and Mother of Pragnya. The interesting dialogue of inquiry self of Savitri with her own discovered higher self is as follows:

She replies to the Mother of Compassion thus:

> "Madonna of suffering, Mother of grief divine, Thou art a portion of my soul put forth
> To bear the unbearable sorrow of the world. Because thou art, men yield not to their doom, But ask for happiness and strive with fate; Because thou art, the wretched still can hope. But thine is the power to solace, not to save.
> One day I will return, a bringer of strength, And make thee drink from the Eternal's cup; His streams of force shall triumph in thy limbs
> And Wisdom's calm control thy passionate heart. Thy love shall be the bond of humankind, Compassion the bright key of Nature's acts: Misery shall pass abolished from the earth;
> The world shall be freed from the anger of the Beast,
> From the cruelty of the Titan and his pain.
> There shall be peace and joy for ever more."

Suffering is real; that reality gave birth to Buddhism. Buddhism has provided succour to many. Yet, suffering endures for a large number of people. Savitri understands that compassion can provide a solace but not the solution. Her resolve is to arrive at that milestone that may provide a final solution. Therefore, she moves forward to Mother of Power.

She comes face to face with Mother of Power; say Devi Durga, yet Savitri knows that power of action is limited for a final dissolution of problems.

To quote Sri Aurobindo,

> "Madonna of might, Mother of works and force,
> Thou art a portion of my soul put forth
> To help mankind and help the travail of Time.
> Because thou art in him, man hopes and dares;
> Because thou art, men's souls can climb the heavens
> And walk like gods in the presence of the Supreme.

> But without wisdom power is like a wind,
> It can breathe upon the heights and kiss the sky,
> It cannot build the extreme eternal things.
> Thou hast given men strength, wisdom thou couldst not give. One day I will return, a bringer of light;
> Then will I give. . . . Thou shalt see self . . .
> Reflected in the bright pool of thy soul.
> Thy wisdom shall be vast as vast thy power. Then hate shall dwell no more in human hearts, And fear and weakness shall desert men's lives, The cry of the ego shall be hushed within,
> Its lion roar that claims the world as food, All shall be might and bliss and happy force."

This spirit is designed so as to protect the unfortunate and save the doomed. It also destroys tyrannical forces.

We shall travel with Savitri towards Mother of Light. However, let us pause to understand how powerful the power of thought is.

A Brief History of the Power of Thought

It is a misconstruction to say that the past is dead and gone. At every point of time when the present is experienced as a fresh and fertile possibility, the past is present by its contributions that have made the present a materialized moment. This awareness of the past as it shaped the present makes the study of history relevant to our understanding of the happenings in the present as well as the portents of the possibilities in the future. All the occurrences as experienced by the mankind that encompass the entire span of the culture and civilization of man—be it philosophy or the physical sciences, be it mathematics or medicine, be it astronomy or astrology, be it the field of fine arts or the sphere of performing arts or for that matter any discipline of scholastic pursuit—have their primordial origin in the form of an idea.

Idea is the first reality. A conglomeration of ideas generates a thought. The thought may translate to a concept. When the concept gathers momentum, with communication, it will reverberate into several, numerous minds. With this happening, there may be a powerful progression of power of thought processes. But let us first begin with a beginning. Before five thousand years, when the Rishis while meditating heard a voice from the sky, it was about a thought that occurred to the Changeless and Formless Reality to manifest itself into multiple forms. Thus, the first thought may be said to have been 'Ekoham Bahusyam'. It was this thought that led to various manifestations of the forms that exist. Or to change the paradigm from the philosophical postulate to scientific jargon, there was a Big Bang and so originated the Universe. The Big Bang is also an idea.

The eastern philosophy had carved out mystic and profound thought forms and elaborated them into subtleties like *smritis, Upanishads, Puranas* in India and *Zen koans* in Japan. They form an ever reverberating symphony of archetypal symbols. Even to those who are far distant, they in some unexplained way, are a kind of a mystic lure.

We cannot but allude, with the risk of a slight diversion to bring an abstract idea such as a thought into actual, physical reality. The technique of how to visualize the Gateway to the power of thought—*Icchashakti*; and, bring the process of thought to actualization—*Kriyashakti* in the physical world. This technique is the heritage of mankind, provided by Kashmir School of Shaivism—*Kashmir Shiva Agama* 1112. Let their tribe flourish.

It is impossible to dwell on the diverse kind of infinite forms that have evolved through imagery of these thoughts but review of a few instances can also be illustrative. From beginning at an indefinite time of moment zero, let us take a quantum jump to about 2500 years ago. As history goes, Rishi Patanjali gathered some 3000 listeners at Chidambaram and taught them a profound process of psychodynamics that would bring about a complete dissolution of mind. Obviously, when there is no mind, where will an idea be? To put it into currency of the present times, it can be described as a masterpiece of unparalleled excellence about the sophisticated software systems in psychodynamics, titled Patanjali *Yoga Sutra*. It is compiled in a bare minimum of one hundred and ninety six aphorisms. Apart from enunciating various forms of psychocybernetics of meditative practices, it provides insight into the observer-observed phenomenon.

Most ideas fail to propel themselves and die in a short while. Historians would look at a thought if it survived more than 60 years. Patanjali creation has survived as a heritage of mankind and it is being studied and pursued both in East and West. Such a long survival can be best cited as an exemplary evidence for survival of the weakest; the weakest survives because of its intrinsic value unpolluted by any self-interest; for the largest benefit of the largest portion of mankind. It still has to strive and not yield before changing the mindset of mankind.

Vigyana-Bhairava teaches over a hundred modalities of psychocybernetic systems in a short treatise. *Shrimad Bhagwatam* has a profoundly rich repertoire of imagery interspersed with time fragmentation and distortion creating a hypnoidal state so conducive for psychotherapeutic isomorphism. What must be the source of intuitive insight of the Rishis of Upanishads who fathomed the depths of mind to say that—mind alone is the cause of bondage and freedom of all men?

Psychiatrists have been trying for a few decades to classify the criteria for Diagnostic and Statistical Manual of Mental Disorders—DSM. It has already changed its form into 5 editions and still further formatting is necessary. Would there be any power in such a process to propel itself all across the world to be uniformly followed? We doubt it for sure.

Another classic instance of persuasive suggestibility of the *Bhagavad Gita* may be cited to convince about the influence of such a masterpiece of therapeutic manipulations not only in struggle and strife of day-to-day life but also in neurotic states. *Gita*, even today moulds the collective consciousness of a large segment of the human race. What a wondrous conceptualization of the psyche is made here when it describes the mind as the sixth sense organ! All the concepts have their origin/cognition in the end, making it the vital sense organ for perception of the world of our own making. It is the sixth sense which indeed secretes ideas.

Or to take the illustration from the Chinese thought, Confucius and Lao Tse certainly did not provide a linear didactic rational exercise for mental manipulations that a rebellion may be brought about. A rebellion or a revolt is a contorted methodology for a radical change. Chinese philosophers extolled the virtue of bending like a bamboo rather than being uprooted as a tall tree. The thought has relevance to survival. There are several empirical evidences in history; we cite a few examples.

- General Mikhail Kutuzov was Commander-in-chief of the Russian Army. When Napoleon invaded Russia in 1812, there was a singular command from Kutuzov, to retreat. Napoleon was lured all the way to Moscow without resistance. He did not realize how outstretched his supplies were and how enfeebled his soldiers were by malaria. In Moscow, Russian army playing on their terms pounced upon the French and Napoleon had to flee facing his first defeat.
- Even better strategic display was shown by Indian Army marching on to Dhaka during the Bangladesh Liberation War. Gen. Sam Manekshaw ordered the Indian Army not to fight Pak resistance in what was at that time Eastern Pakistan, now Bangladesh. His strategy was based on the ways of meandering waters of the rivers of the region, such as, Brahmaputra, Meghna, Padma and others. The river waters changed their path when encountered with

obstacles. Rather than fighting the resistance of several Pak army units, Indian Army decided to circumvent the loci of resistance and move closer to Dhaka. This provided a fast forward march to Dhaka and resulted in the largest ever surrender of an army comprising about 95,000 soldiers including their commander-in-chief. Finally, it was the power of a fragile lady, Indira Gandhi. She emerged as Durga incarnate, destroyer of all that is evil. Maybe the thought was provided by the poetry of Rabindranath Tagore. And, Sword was wielded for sure by Gen. Maneckshaw but neither of them would have been able to do what they accomplished without the movement of a powerful hand of Durga, not only with power but with wisdom as well. In the name of religion, what great injustice was inflicted upon the gentle, kind, poetry loving Bangladeshis! After liberation, one of the main tasks of the emerged nation was to abort unwanted embryos following rape by Pak soldiers.

- In the same vein, Tibetan Buddhism advocated for reconciliation of the conflict by meeting at the Midway—the Middle Way approach adopted by the Dalai Lama as of now. The relevance has to be judged by the results. When one side keeps on walking all the time up to the Middle Way, as the Dalai Lama seems to have done, it is not difficult that when the other side has not moved at all, the Middle Way of action will land the adversary at the feet of the opponent. Indeed some brand these philosophers as counter-revolutionaries, including some Tibetan youth.

Judging by the results, Communism has vastly demonstrated the power of thought. It successfully divided the world into two blocs for a long time.

Those who rely exclusively on didactic logistics would wish to forcefully destroy existing order to bring about a revolutionary change. But a little reflection would show that advocates of this thought process would be practically ineffective in the present time. Once upon a time, it was thought that the next war would be fought with ICBMs—Intercontinental Ballistic Missiles. As of now, the war between Israel and Hamas witnessed mid air destruction of 300 missiles fired from Hamas to Israel. Long before, the USA and USSR realized the futility of amassing large scale atomic weapons. Today, no nuclear power will dare to fire the first atom bomb since it will amount to a huge war crime.

Instead a subtlety to exercise the power seems to be emerging with an altogether different approach. It does not show the hand which fires the weapon and yet innumerable weapons that multiply on their own happen to disable the entire world population such as Corona virus.

Would there be such a powerful thought that would not think of an individual personal gain but would want every gift of Nature to be shared equitably by the entire mankind? Environmentalists engage into confrontation where they see violation that will endanger the source. If they succeed in waging a long fight, they celebrate their success by dedicating it to everyone since environment is not an exclusive privilege to a person, to a class, or society. It belongs to everyone. It subtly elaborates a gentle methodology full of tenderness and suppleness based on intuitive approaches of the right brain experiences that can bring about a transformation through metamorphosis. Intuitive wisdom seems to arise from deeper depths of the unconscious mind. Accumulated wisdom after dwelling and diving deep into the unconscious processes takes a long time to articulate into speech and action. However, when they do so eventually, a moment reveals what ages have toiled to express. Let us make gentle progress.

Thought processes do have a relativistic transformation. When a thesis is at its peak, it is postulated that the birth of anti-thesis has already occurred. This takes discursive dialectics with progressive discussions that is likely to bring about synthesis. A new thesis is thus born. That is how each and every civilization has made progress. Concept of wisdom arising out of Pragnya has been virtually copied and repeated without any progression. The present exposition aims to take the concept in a fast forward mode so that not only does psychology earn an additional point to be classed as a science but a scientific measuring tool with mathematics involved also evolves.

- Vagaries of human situations have motivated thinkers to find novel solutions. Novel ideas are fanciful and attract kind, compassionate individuals to support them. Friedrich Engels was such a person who funded Karl Marx to write *Das Kapital* while sitting in London, capital of Imperialist Britain. And did not even Karl Marx, after advocating class conflict as the only way to solve the human issues to bring about the dictatorship of the proletariat rely on the subtlety of natural phenomena to anticipate that the state would eventually wither away. Probably not even Karl Marx himself could imagine that the power of his thoughts would grip the entire world. Super-States came into existence by his call to the proletariat for the revolt as they had "nothing to lose but your chains" by doing so. But casting off the chains caused a paradoxical loss of freedom. The state did not wither away. Instead, it had absolute power, corrupting the powerful absolutely. There is no count to those who have toiled the most of their lives or faced death in communist camps. He was astonished that Marxists propelled communist ideology with colossal atrocities. He is said to have exclaimed, "Thank God, I am not a Marxist!" Who could have prognosticated except the mystical philosophers with intuitive insights into the cravings of the souls—like Rohit Mehta in 1935—that Soviet Union is bound to collapse? The prophecy did come true for Soviet Union. Can it be said that it can also happen for Communist China? The evidence as of now is on the contrary. Yet, hope lurks eternally in the human breast—let us include even the Chinese. We can deduce evidence as to how this will happen.

HOPE

↓

Liberty **Equalilty** **Fraternity**

This inspired the French Revolution about 200+ years ago. That justifies France to be the first republic nation. The ideals are now universal aspirations for entire humanity.

↓

Only 2 per cent of Chinese population need to foster idealistically and deep in their heart, they do believe. Justification for this equation is empirical evidence provided by Mahesh yogi—TM guru.

He arrived at a quasi-physical-mathematical formula that 7000 persons were needed to meditate. This was in 1982. Mathematical basis was derived by calculating total population on the earth and again taking it to some algorithm as to arrive at 7000 people. These numbers of brains radiating peace, kindness, compassion in synchrony produce a gigantic field by their convergence.

That produces conscilience. That is a new term for the phrase—Communion in consciousness/convergence on a single idealistic thought such as hope. Empirical evidence was provided by researchers that after the experiment was conducted, there was evidence across the world that there was no war and peace prevailed for about 21 days.

Following this kind of lead provided by Roger Nelson, he formulated a worldwide network of dedicated computers that will monitor upsurge or downtrend of conscilience.

Shirley Telles at Swami Vivekanand Yoga Anusthan Sansthan, Bangalore, noticed upsurge in conscilience during Ramzan, at the time of a *soma yagna*, during the high mass of the Infant Jesus feast, at a meeting of social workers (*pracharak*) at Prashanti Kutiram (from the RSS), before/at midnight on New Year's eve (Indian Time). There appeared to be a convergence of noble thoughts within the minds of numerous individuals so as to produce a coherence that can be detected on a computer. Bottom line is that happenings do happen, regardless whether any one is there to record them.

Edgar Cayce was the chief investigator on the USA side during the cold war years. The USA and USSR both were using disinformation techniques, sending messages to and fro that they have mastered the technique of probing the mind without any personal contact. Cayce confirmed personally that both sides finally agreed, *what a hoax it was!* Empirical evidence is the currency of present times. Yet, Nature keeps on doing natural work. How it will find expression, only time will tell.

It is pertinent, even at a cost of small deviation from the main theme, to ponder as to what forces in nature are likely to change the brutal ways of communist ideology to radical humanism. We cite only one subtlety in human psyche, viz. fundamental appetite of the soul, freedom, liberty and equality. These were the forces that propelled the French Revolution. This thought may progress in linear logistic method of deduction and induction, therefore, it is indeed the grammar of thought process.

- Rene Descartes perfected this process of reasoning where it was axiomatic to look for mechanistic connection between the cause and effect like the gears of a clock. His visionary singular statement that *Cogito, Ergo Sum* —I think, therefore, I am—classically illustrates how the wisdom of centuries of thought processes can be expressed in a single sentence. Different thinkers will expound the depth of this statement in several ways and when the expounded boundaries find limitations, it is likely that the misinterpretation may prevail.

- Development of modern medicine is classic empirical evidence. This has progressed by providing evidence based solutions. The process erred when it forgot to include the thinker as one of the parameters. Scientific methodology has this inherent virtue that it accepts that mistakes may occur with fallacious reasoning provided by prejudicial thought. The authors belong to the present generation of surgeons. They are a living testimony to a colossal mistake committed by modern medicine. There occurs an ulcer in duodenum. Duodenum is the first part of the small intestine that comes in contact with gastric contents. Gastric juice is secreted by gastric mucosa where one of the contents is hydrochloric acid. Levels of hydrochloric acid are variable in subjects. When some patients were found to have a coincidental occurrence of high level of hydrochloric acid and duodenal ulcer, it was accepted that peptic ulcer was caused by a high level of acid in gastric juice. Alas! What a tragedy! A coincidence was accepted and larger and larger portions of the stomach were sacrificed to remove acid secreting mucosa. It was equivalent to hanging an innocent person! Eventually, two Australian general practitioners, Barry Marshall and Robin Warren, demonstrated that not hydrochloric acid but a bacterium now called as H. Pylori was the causative organism!!! This is amenable to treatment with antibiotics etc. No surgery needed—Aha!

But poetry is seldom written through the medium of grammar. The quantum jump in thought is akin to poetic inspiration; occurring in spurts, going through a cyclical process based on the *yin-yang* principle. This proclaims an antithesis for every thesis that is postulated; their conflict eventually resolving into a synthesis.

- Shining empirical evidence is provided by Jain philosophy. Anekantavada is a school of philosophy. It postulates an endless cycle of ever changing paradigm shifts. This was propounded by Mahavir, the last of the 24 Jain *Tirthankaras* as they are called. Cyclic process of thesis against antithesis giving rise to a new thesis by synthesis is a well charted psychodynamic process across civilizations. The bottom line rests when a practitioner of this philosophy accepts that there is no finality. This automatically leads to another axiomatic philosophical precept of Jain tradition—syada vada. The Jain philosophy at once proclaims its finiteness through syada vada—measure of relativistic existence or progression. This, in practice, limits the value of all principles, including even ethics. Each situation has to be determined on its relative value of benefit and loss. Practice of Jain religion entails extreme penance. This is unlikely for most people. This limited the number of Jain followers to a few. But, considering each and every transaction only on the benefit to be derived therefrom —for business community benefits equate financial gain —has provided the Jain community with a very powerful flexibility to manipulate ethical values and flourish.

Howsoever, undeciphered the causality maybe, sometimes it brings about a mutatic change which is neither metamorphosis nor transformation. In such an instance, the new idea has severed its direct linkage to the predecessor and exists now in a form that has never been before. This is a stupendous phenomenon which may even be compared to a quantum jump.

The mutations do not necessarily conform to their original virtuosity. As an antithesis to good, truth, knowledge, wisdom and bliss, not only does evil exist but is already born when the positivity is at its crest. Thus, the Platonic ideals of humanism, excellence, versatility, rational orderliness, beauty, vitality, hope and love are counterpoised by ruse, cunning hatred, avarice, artifice, conspiracy, sickness, suffering, destruction, death, devastation and war. By a relentless inquiry into what men think they know, by asserting that man is the real measure of all things and proclaiming that unexamined life is not worth living, people at large and the rulers may be so disturbed that Socrates may be compelled to drink poison.

- Platonic ideas as shadows of reality to the chained men inside the cave may indeed reflect to metamorphose into Machiavellian politics. Thus, Chanakyaniti also finds its anti-thesis in Charvakaniti. At such an intersection, we are left wondering about the isomorphism of the ideas across centuries. What was the linkage in consciousness between Adi Shankara and Plato for both of them to visualize the world of appearances as shadows—maya? Why and how similar ideas occur to thinkers without any physical connection? Is there a matrix of knowledge that is pervading all over, like Wi-Fi today, simply to be plugged into so that ideas flow into thoughts and find expression? Is there indeed a Universal Mind—of the Vedantic concept and Jungian elucidation and Roger Sperry's annotation which identifies consciousness as the ultimate unresolved mystery—that leaves engrams on the cerebral cortex not only in an individual cerebral cortex but also on the collective consciousness of the mankind? These are futuristic questions for research.

The evil may thus be an antithesis and so, existing by its own right or it may be an aberration from good which one may like to be a natural state of thought. In any case, almost all individuals pursue goals that they think are good for them.

- Seeing the subjective reality of self-security as the fundamental foundation of selfhood. Freud conceptualized ego as a psychic self constantly striving to balance the conflicting super-ego and id. Ego may be able to ascertain enlightened self-interest and bring about reconciliation; often the desire equates with personal good and its denial as evil. The stress and strife to maintain equipoise in such a situation may become too much to cope with. Then it is fascinating and yet at the same time a saddening experience to observe the deviation of thought in the form of neurotic compensations (see Ch.-7: Mind is like a mirror). However, prevalent neurosis may be, even Freud accepted the possibility to mature into a reality that may serve better purpose. He has included sublimation also as a process. Sublimation of powerful sex drive is also feasible. Numerous empirical evidences are evident with saints of various traits. Going a step further, sublimation of self-interest may mature into altruism—the goal will be the largest good of the largest number.
- It is a sad fact of human existence that the thinkers get tormented by their own creations—ideas. What a pathetic paradox it is that the self-destructive trait is most evident in highly creative individuals! The suicide rates are highest among the Nobel laureates—what magnificent personalities were people like John Fitzgerald, Arthur Koestler or Ernest Hemingway! Whatever may be the compulsions or their reasons or neurosis, the forcible elimination of a beautiful unfolding is shocking. It is even more traumatic when such termination is brought from outside, as is the case of Mahatma Gandhi or Leon Trotsky or Martin Luther King. When the philosophers amongst such creative personalities like Vinoba Bhave and several Jain saints, find a subtle way for a final exit that corresponds with the classic death wish, to die like a ripe

fruit being automatically detached from a plant, it is some solace compared to traumatic expulsions.

- Even something bad contributes, Rabindranath Tagore sang, "A deep distress has humanized my soul." (Chapter 4: Deep Distress has Humanized my Soul). Suffering and sorrow did make a Buddha out of Siddhartha, and through the choice of the middle path, Buddhism proclaimed four noble truths basic to good thoughts as, "know the suffering, give up their causes, attend to the cessation of suffering and follow the true path: also charting out the details of the pathway in very simple and rational thought as, "right views, right intentions, right speech, right action, right living, right effort, right mindfulness and right conversation". Through the repetition of such a basic formula for balancing psychodynamics, Buddhist psychology flowered into giving thousands of programs for meditative reflections. Buddhist programs were certain and specific like the causality and change: one should practice samata meditation to generate equanimity: meditation on metta or Avalokitesvara would enhance the quality of compassion and so on to the pinnacle of Kalachakra meditation where the practitioner imbibes the virtues and the qualities of nine hundred and twenty eight pious forms.
- If this is spanned across to a time bridge of 2500 years, Hans Selye pioneered the research on stress response linking it to neurotransmitters and endocrines only in 1936 and Candace Pert began the discovery of the information substances only in early 1970s. When the scientists have discovered these phenomena it is but natural that the physiological function of the body may be viewed as the working of an interactive, reverberating, cybernetic chemical model. The philosophical concepts of the mind being the originator of health/disease,

then, may also be translated to biochemical events. The chemical basis of short/long term memory, of the conditioned reflexes and stress response is already well deciphered. We have a blueprint of biochemical profile of how state dependent memory and learning leave their imprints not only on the autonomic nervous system and endocrine glands but also on the immune system. The brain is the largest endocrine gland not only by size but by its secretion of numerous information substances directly into the bloodstream. Potent substances like corticotropin, growth hormones, thyrotropin, prolactin, chronic gonadotropin, encephalins, vasoactive intestinal peptides and somatostatin are now found to be located in the immune competent cells and are therefore labeled as cytokines. These cells apart from being carriers may even be producing these information substances. That means there are innumerable thoughts floating as particles in the bloodstream.

Generally, the principle of homeostasis prevails. But, as is evident during Coronavirus infection, several cytokines may be secreted at once so as to produce a cytokine storm. The defense system itself may contribute to mortality. Cytokine storm will involve a sudden large scale secretion of several active molecular substances. Their discussion will involve sophisticated science including bioinformatics. That is out of relevance here.

The brain, through the limbic system, influences secretion of the cytokines. The limbic system, in turn, is activated by the psychic events—thought. Mind-brain linkage is thus established. The brain-body connection is through the chain influence of the limbic system, hypothalamus and pituitary gland on the thymus, spleen and lymph nodes apart from effects on autonomic nervous system and endocrine glands. All of them cause secretion of the cytokines with wide ranging effects, including cybernetic feedback to the brain.

The cytokines thus may indeed be considered circulating thought particles in the bloodstream which apart from several effects on diverse systems, may depress and also enhance the immune system. In any case Aldous Huxley[12] now need not resort to smoking marijuana or ask for the development of a wonderful pill that may engineer a psychedelic experience of Buddhahood in the Nonself that was the chair as painted by Van Gogh.

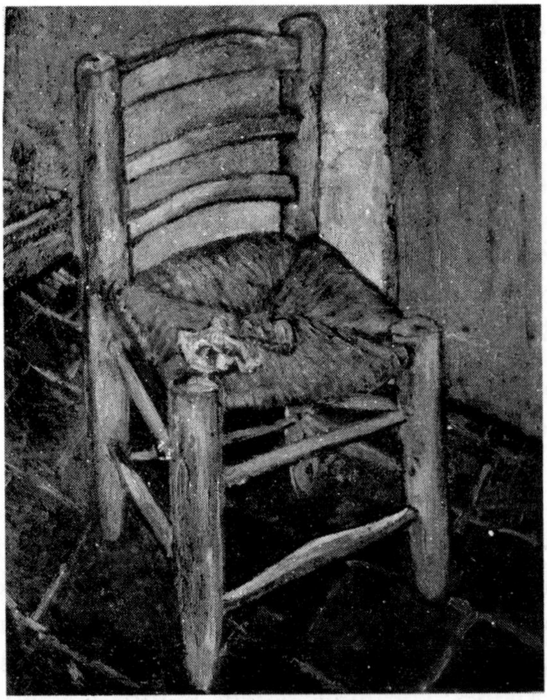

Van Gogh's The Chair

We now have the intricate knowledge of the abundant storehouses of memory and related capabilities that are there in the brain, endocrine glands, at the synapses, in the reticulo-endothelial systems and circulating cells in the blood that almost provide particles for each thought form. What an exciting revelation it is that long, long before we have such information; several software systems in psychology for such a transduction were already evolved and widely practiced.

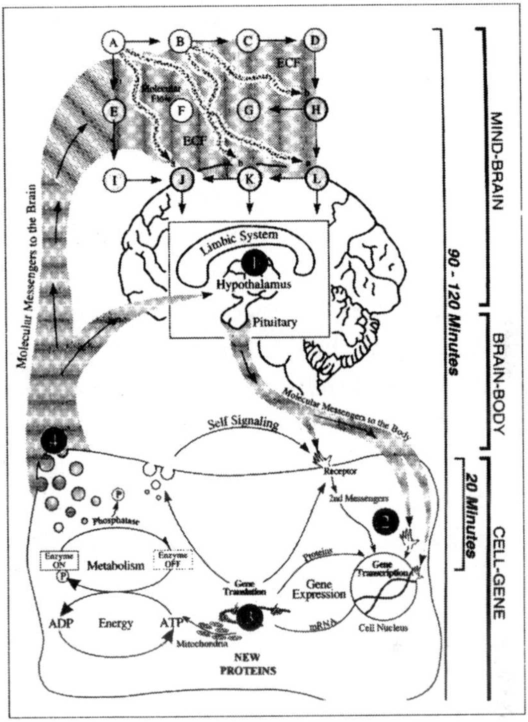

Source: The USA Psychotherapy Journal, Vo. 3, No. 2: 30-49 (2004).

- And these systems have vistas even beyond what can be grasped through modern modality of science. Quantum physics specified the observer-observed phenomena whereby in every act of experimentation—observation—the observer became an integral part of the observation; there is no way yet, in material sciences, whereby we may eliminate the observer to arrive at a truly objective reality. On the other hand, psychodynamics for elimination of the observer from the mind was prescribed by Eastern tradition through various methods of meditation.

Thus, there may be a true freedom of choice as the pragmatists like Jean Paul Sartre envisaged. Revolutions were engineered through subtle idealism.

Thus, mechanisms of the mind do indeed keep on creating various forms of bondage and generating aspirations for liberation from them. And mankind is indeed gifted through the phenomenon of occurrence of people with abundant wisdom, Bodhisattvas—beings that constantly strive to alleviate the sufferings of their fellow-men. Their creative geniuses constantly formulate software programs for enhancing joy and happiness. The master manipulators of psyche like Erik Erikson, Milton Erikson, William Roger, Eric Fromm and several others have given us such refined and well-crafted software systems whereby many are inspired and encouraged to try the therapeutic use of programs to alleviate and mitigate human suffering arising out of psychological disorders. J. Krishnamurthy named the software as the Nameless experience. This is typical of his inimitable style of teaching without giving references.

- Yet artistic application being the work of an individual's creative upsurge, only a few are likely to be able to provide freedom from the shackles of distorted thought that masters so easily achieved: yet the aspiration to master and the persistence to achieve even an incidental success are natural dues of all those who in words of Romain Rolland strive, struggle, not to find and yet not to yield.
- If we were to discover freedom in some form of bondage as Tagore did, a permanent riddance of the cyclical change may be possible. For that, a poetic experience of love, whose sweet and serene bondage the artist in Rabindranath finds freedom is a privilege of all but availed of by only a fortunate few. The expression of love may take innumerable aesthetic forms; of beauty, of serene sublimity, of caring for the fragile and vulnerable, of

compassion for fellow sufferers and so on. Schopenhauer indeed found an escape from the unavoidable bondage of existence by experiencing love for the human race as "my fellow sufferers" in a pathetic drama where entry and exit were not of one's own choice; thus making the play a definite tragedy.

And yet, human aspirations as they have been from primordial times, will not accept the finality in the form of tragedy. In the most abject despair, there is a latent possibility for the generation of new psychological software design which can bring about the descent of the grace. There has been a constant yearning for the ascent on the pathways of thought and beyond thought. Seers, like Sri Aurobindo, have time and again sanctified the generation of intuitive insights when a moment reveals what ages toiled to express.

Such bliss would always remain a spiritual experience, so subtle and yet so immense that it will always be unquantifiable. And it may indeed be the human destiny to build the high temples of aesthetics and beauty in the forms of various thoughts that encompass not only our culture and civilization but every form of human endeavor. The lamps of hope and aspiration will continue to be lighted through the fire of faith. Whether the temple will be consecrated or the ideas were merely ghosts in the mind or whether there was a design for discovering scientific innovations; no one will ever be able to decipher. The journey through the history of power of thought along with the fourth dimension of time and space through the ride along with various thought forms, thus can indeed be a rough roller coaster ride. At times exhilarating and at times frightening. But the thinkers as the humans are made to be, a ride is a must. There shall be no use to the power of thought unless it is shared. Life is based on societal relationships that have evolved by a progression to the present state. One is indeed fortunate to have some camaraderie at a few intersections which not only fosters the joy of comradeship but reduces fears. Having had the privilege of intersecting with so many genuine thinkers, we must acknowledge our gratitude for the shared insights with friends, philosophers and guides. Though they were genuine mentors who mended our personality and melted our ego, they persistently persuaded us not to acknowledge them as gurus.

But apart from the gratuitous graces, the journey is indeed, from alone to Alone. Journey alone is not only arduous but is surmounted with difficulties. A constantly occurring question is how to verify the actions as true. In such situations, there is no mentor, no guru, maybe only fingers pointing the path forward. When one is face to face with that Alone, there is no need to verify, to judge, to rationalize. Courage of conviction arising out of wisdom is a subtle and sure guide. What would the metaphor that 'there are only fingers pointing the path' mean? The indications accrue from poetic wisdom as sung by Sri Aurobindo.

The fable takes Savitri beyond the Madonna of Power; may be called Durga. Savitri refuses to be cajoled even by the Mother of Power and she does not want a compromise: She wants a final resolution. She has to proceed to that pragmatic wisdom which may be an intuitive insight to understand good and bad as well as discriminate between noble and evil. That light can only be endowed upon Savitri when she sees the incarnation of her real self. She moves on to proceed towards the Mother of Light that is Pragnya. Let us once again take recourse to splendid depiction by Sri Aurobindo as:

> "Madonna of light, Mother of joy and peace,
> Thou art a portion of my self put forth
> To raise the spirit to its forgotten heights
> And wake the soul by touches of the heavens.
> Because thou art, the soul draws near to God;
> Because thou art, love grows in spite of hate
> And knowledge walks unslain in the pit of Night.
> But not by showering heaven's golden rain
> Upon the intellect's hard and rocky soil
> Can the tree of Paradise flower on earthly ground . . .
>
> Even if thou rain down intuition's rays,
> The mind of man will think it earth's own gleam,
> His spirit by spiritual ego sink,
> Or his soul dream shut in sainthood's brilliant cell
> Where only a bright shadow of God can come.
> His hunger for the eternal thou must nurse
> And fill his yearning heart with heaven's fire
> And bring God down into his body and life.

Savitri has already identified her sacred self. It is a composite of compassion, power, and light that is wisdom. She has understood that compassion without power will be only a cry in the wilderness.

Power without wisdom is like a blind drunken man who is running amok. He would have no direction and would be likely to wound an entire civilization. Recourse to salvation can arise when wisdom prevails over the entire domain of triple forces.

Sri Aurobindo wrote the epic in a state of poetic trance. To put it in his own words, he said,

> "I used *Savitri* as a means of ascension. I began with it on a certain mental level, each time I could reach a

> higher level I rewrote from that level. . . . In fact *Savitri* has not been regarded by me as a poem to be written and finished, but as a field of experimentation to see how far poetry could be written from one's own yogic consciousness and how that could be made creative."

The poet has used the phrase 'yogic consciousness' that is always a prerogative of poets. They achieve sublimity in such a state when Pragnya would be shining bright.

Sri Aurobindo used the word 'ascension' that has been misunderstood as rising high in a physical level. In the cosmos, there are distances but height and levels are relative. Sri Aurobindo postulated that eventually the entire mankind may achieve a level of height where the grace as wisdom will descend from somewhere. Such a grace has been explored as the Miracle of Descent.

Whether such a miracle is only a mirage that has been dreamt by a poet or not is not pertinent for discussion over here. For each individual, the level of wisdom can be ascended into a better understanding of world order and natural laws.

Above is the most appropriate, poignant portrayal of the concept of Pragnya. Its relevance is doubly empowered since it is the vision by a poet, writing in the stage of ascension into Yogic consciousness. It is pertinent to note that Sri Aurobindo writing in prose, a magnum opus, as *Life Divine* does not mention Pragnya or other such sublime qualities of human intelligence such as compassion and power.[13]

The difficulty arises because psychology has only recently emerged as a science. Few years before Freud, there was synonymy between psychology and philosophy. Now even the boundaries of philosophy are well defined, yet, a standard vocabulary as well as a dictionary of psychological words is yet to emerge. This will definitely be so in a short while.

Let us now take recourse to contemporary times. Empirical evidence cited as being personally witnessed.

- Dalai Lama is said to be the 14th incarnation of Avalokitesvara, i.e. compassionate Buddha form. The Dalai Lama has sung:

  "To alleviate the sufferings of humanity I shall be born again and again . . ."

The Dalai Lama is duty bound to protect Tibetan people. As a sovereign, he was too young to be effective. Chinese, led by Mao Tsetung and the wily Zhou-Enlai (Tibetans called him Mr. Chew and Lie) wanted the Dalai Lama, Tenzing Gyatso, to be in their possession and undergo indoctrination as per communist ideology. Young Dalai Lama had to flee from Tibet.

Though he was recognized as a deported sovereign person by the Government of India for several years, the Dalai Lama relinquished the throne and devolved the Supreme Authority to Tibetan people. Yet, the Dalai Lama through his wise counsel has influenced the lives of millions of people across the globe; authors included.

In a personal handwritten note to the authors, he expressed that someday his wisdom will also prevail over the Chinese.

- The power of thought is best illustrated as to how the pen is mightier than the sword. Carl Marx wrote his magnum opus, *Das Kapital.* Never did he realize that his book was to divide the world into powerful blocs. The USA and USSR started stockpiling nukes to the extent that the globe can be destroyed several times. Fortunately, wisdom prevails now. Yet, out of fear about the opponent being foolish, there are several nuclear nations now.
- Disintegration of the USSR was engineered by a few powerful persons such as the then Pope and the then President of the USA. The motivating force was to dwell

upon the fact that freedom is a fundamental appetite of the soul. A small nation, Poland, was the first to lead with labour leader Lech Walesa. Russian people were led by Gorbachev. They uprooted the giant statue of Lenin.

This is massive empirical evidence that power of thought prevails.

- Radha Bernier was elected as President of International Theosophical Society for several consecutive terms and remained as President for nearly half a century. She was a spiritual head of Esoteric Society as well. The Society is spread world-wide.

She was asked how she could maintain her equipoise—steadiness of Pragnya. Her reply was,

> "Being at the helm of affairs, the organization is bound to involve interaction with numerous people. It was unavoidable that some politics also creeped in. Politics involves who should get what, when, why and how?
> I have to remain astute.
> Those who benefited from my action praised me. I was not extolled. Those who desire to have some benefit, but were found lacking, cursed me with favouritism.
> I was not to be derided. I was doing my duty.
> I have a special relationship with my Masters. That is sacred. Cannot be discussed in open but I remain answerable to them all the time."

- J. Krishnamurti was asked, "Why is your teaching so purely psychological? There is no cosmology, no theology, no ethics, no aesthetics, no sociology, not even hygiene. Why do you concentrate only on the mind and its workings?"

K: Sir, most of us live everyday life with mental manipulations. Mind is an operational instrument all the time. Sages are very very few. Therefore, most of the problems arise when people see difficult situations different from their way of liking. If the thinker can understand himself, then the whole problem is solved. Then he is creation; he is reality; and then what he does will not be antisocial.

Virtue is not an end in itself; virtue brings freedom, and there can be freedom only when the thinker, which is the mind, ceases.

Q: During your lifetime, there were two World Wars. What is your specific contribution?

K: Wars first arise in the minds of men. That is why I constantly emphasize on serenity of mind.

- During the times of Emergency in India, Prime Minister Indira Gandhi had a one-to-one meeting with J. Krishnamurthy. After coming out, she was seen with tears flowing from her eyes.

Soon thereafter, she revoked the Emergency and declared an election.

- Rohit Mehta was a free thinking philosopher. He explored several vistas from East and West and Africa as well. He remained a confirmed theosophist for namesake upto his lifetime. Sardar Vallabhbhai Patel saw him seated in a front row at one of his meetings at Varanasi after independence. He had known Rohit as a young man, a maverick, a mustang and a rebel. Mahatma Gandhi wrote to young Rohit once every week while he was in prison. Sardar Patel invited Rohit Mehta to move to Delhi. It was his natural due since he had fought for India's freedom. Position of power did not lure Rohit Mehta. He was satisfied with himself teaching across India and elsewhere in the world.

There is no litmus test for wisdom. People shine out with merit when they act wise. And wisdom is not an exclusive prerogative for any caste, creed or race. Nature distributes wisdom equitably, however, only a select few individuals have a chance to show it with their performance. We have cited only a few instances where we had a personal brush with such wise people. On the other hand, several Socrates have been poisoned—killed by competitors across the world. Eulogy can only be sung for the illustrious.

Notes

1. *Rig-Veda* Shlokas ||२.३.९||
2. *Rig-Veda* Shloka ||३.२९.१६||
3. *Cha.Sa.* Sutra Sthana 11/43.
4. Essence of Yogavaashistha—Compiled by Shri Jnanananda Bharati.
5. Indian Handbook of Hypnotherapy Foundations and Strategies, Ch. 1,—Dr. Rajni & Dr. Bhaskar Vyas.
6. *Patanjali Yoga Sutra,* Chapter 2, Verse 27.
7. *Patanjali Yoga Sutra,* Chapter 1, Verse 48.
8. *Bhagavad Gita,* Chapter 2, verse 54-58.
9. *Bhagavad Gita,* Chapter 6, verse 17.
10. *Shiva Tandava Stotra.*
11. *Vijñâna-bhairava-tantra—7th Century CE.*
12. *The Doors of Perception,* 1954, Aldous Huxley.
13. *Psychology in the Indian Tradition*—Anand Paranjpe, K. Ramakrishna Rao.

4
Deep Distress has Humanized my Soul

An inevitable outcome of vitiated perception propelling the action is suffering. It can be self-inflicted or inflicted on the people around. Having had exposure to the concept of Pragnya, we shall now look into some of the facets that can be distorted. A common factor to almost all the people distorting Pragnya is to have suffered. An acute suffering would surely be mitigated with time; however, aggrievement may last for a long duration. Eventually, most people cope with the situation and move on to the task ahead in life. A byproduct surely and certainly accrues during the process. That is where compassion arises deep within the heart and endures for a lifetime. This by itself can be a rekindling of Pragnya. That is how Rabindranath Tagore sang 'a deep distress has humanized my soul'. We shall elaborate as follows:

The universal truth is one which is timeless and changeless. It is the basis of the processes in nature. It is eminent by itself. The statements describing it tend to be remarkably brief. One would, therefore, expect the understanding of the statement to be easy and self-explanatory. In practice what we observe is to the contrary. Shankaracharya's statement about the nature of ultimate reality is one such example. He stated that the Brahman alone is real and the rest is an illusion. The incomplete understanding and the misinterpretation of this statement about the eternal truth has caused considerable confusion. It has come to be misinterpreted that the entire life process as we see it on this earth is devoid of any meaning. It was postulated that Shankara refers to some other world of reality. A natural corollary was the belief that if this world is an illusion, then our joys and sorrows, pleasures and pain, compassion and suffering are all unreal. The conclusion is in sharp contrast to our everyday experience. Such a paradoxical situation has created a conflict in the minds of the scholars and the seekers. A person in quest of eternal truth went all the way from the West to Varanasi, India.

There, he comes across the concept of maya, postulating the unreality of the world as we observe it. He asks the professor whether the sufferings of the victims of atomic explosions at Nagasaki and Hiroshima were unreal. When the professor replied in the affirmative, the inquirer found the colossal paradox far too difficult to fathom. The dilemma defied resolution causing him a mental breakdown. If such a cryptic statement leads to a near insane state of the seeking mind, it is little wonder that this concept may cause tremendous confusion in the way of living.

There is a story about Shankara himself. Once a wild elephant tried to attack him. He started running away. Someone remarked to Shankara that the elephant was an illusion and why he was running away from it. Shankara did not stop his attempt to escape the danger. He replied that not only was the mad elephant an illusion but also his running away from it.

Another misleading concept is that of the karmic connection. When it states that one cannot escape from the result of one's action. It would follow that the suffering experienced now is a consequence of some action performed earlier. And it has to be endured. While this is so, it does not necessarily enjoin that human will and effort has no place. However, it has often been misconstrued that the suffering was inevitable and the compassion therefore was meaningless.

Is there a solution to the paradox? Or is it that the fundamental postulates are incorrect? The resolution of the conflict is not so difficult.

Classical Indian tradition described the nature of ultimate reality as blissful joy. On the other hand every sentient being perceives pain as unpleasant and attempts to escape it. The nature of the universe is to be blissful. Leaving this philosophical postulate aside, primary biological responses as experienced by everyone, are to shun away from painful stimuli. This should naturally generate empathy for those who are exposed to suffering and separated from Joy. The feeling of empathy by itself can be a step towards the realisation that all unitary manifestations of consciousness are in reality one. Such a perception of the suffering is an enriching experience. It unites man to man.

It should not however end up in extolling the suffering itself. As empirical evidence from historical times, King Ashok waged a devastating war. The destruction and death subjected him to profound anguish. The savage conqueror was humanised and was converted into a spiritual king. But it would be absurd to suggest that in order to have such a spiritual experience every one must enter into a terrible war.

The classical Indian tradition therefore negates the pleasure and pain principle as a guiding parameter. However, it does exhort the virtue of Tapa, meaning thereby austerity in life.

An austere way of life may not only involve simplicity but fasting also. There are stories that 'Tapa' was one of the standard ways to expiate and please god. Following the exemplary model of Devi Parvati, Hindu girls practice fasting for a few days every year.

Mahatma Gandhi's recourse to fast for long periods is now a historical legend. Whenever he passed through a tumultuous phase of Himalayan conflicts which defied resolution, his standard practice was to take recourse to fasting. His own explanation was that the suffering as a consequence of fasting purified him.

The Jain belief is also somewhat similar. They practice severe penance. While Jainism also believes in the law of Karma, it is thought that one can escape from the bondage of action by suffering voluntarily. A few saints in Jain tradition have taken suffering by fasting to the extreme end—they fast unto death. The aim is to escape from the bondage of living!

Romain Rolland collaborates this view with, "Every blow that makes me bleed, breaks a bond".

This hypothesis invokes an interesting question. Why do some saints who claim to be realized souls, suffer from physical ailments?

As the Christian belief postulates the redemption of mankind through the suffering of Christ, the Indian tradition considers this to be an ongoing process. The enlightened beings are constantly in tiff with Reality. However, being united with their fellow beings through love, they do not aspire for Moksha-freedom from rebirth. Instead, they take upon themselves the suffering of the ailing humanity. So, some saints have taken recourse to hypothesize that their physical ailments happen to come to their physical self by taking away from others.

Perception of the pain is at a mental level. One need not be an accomplished yogi to divert the mind from the body. The self (I, the seer) can similarly be separated from the mind. Such accomplishment is a by-product of a meditative process. It can be achieved through hypnosis. To the enlightened beings the burden of the physical pain at the level of physical self can therefore be no trouble. The Instance of Raman Maharishi is well-known. He had cancer of the arm bone. While the doctors and the onlookers thought that he should be having tremendous pain, he went on doing chores without being least bothered. When the surgery was performed he went through it without any anaesthesia.

J. Krishnamurthy had cancer of Pancreas. A man, who has been a world teacher and who has renounced all bondages, why should he suffer? The reconciliation may be derived from the lyrical statement of Sri Aurobindo.

> "He who would bring the heavens here
> Must descend himself into clay
> And burden of earthly nature bear
> And tread the dolorous way."

The physical pain is thus an identifying factor with all the sentient beings. We all are united by the fact that we all can and do suffer. This concept may appear identical with Schopenhauer.

He has said, "It is absurd to look upon the enormous amount of pain that abounds everywhere originating in needs and necessities, as serving no purpose at all and the result of a mere chance. Without misfortune, men would present the spectacle of unbridled folly, say they would go mad. A ship without a ballast is unstable and would not go straight."

However, Schopenhauer is pessimistic and beyond being a ballast, does not see any further meaning or elevation of consciousness through pain.

The Indian view is not so pessimistic. There is an upward transmigration of the consciousness of all beings. Those who are far advanced on the path revert back to take along with them the trailing fellow beings. Shri Ramakrishna Paramhansa had a growth in his neck. That prevented him from taking any food. The disciples and the followers pleaded with him to cure himself with yogic powers or medicines. He insisted that the tumour and the pain served him to identify himself as a common man.

When he saw anguish and disbelief amongst the most in the gathering, he asked for some food. What he was not able to do for days, people saw him easily doing now. But at the same time there was an experience of satiety amongst all who observed. The followers not only understood but had the experience of universal consciousness.

The Buddhist concept of the Bodhisattvas is identical. The Bodhisattvas take birth again and again with an aim to help the suffering humanity. In the process, they even give up their quest for their Buddhahood and return to the material world. Dalai Lama, according to Tibetan Buddhism doctrine, is one such Bodhisattva, being the quintessence of all-compassionate Avalokiteshwar. He is reborn to uplift not only the people of Tibet but the whole world. This concept finds reinforcement in *Bhagavad Gita* also. Krishna says that he is born again and again to protect the good and to destroy the evil. Sri Aurobindo poetically describes this phenomenon as,

> "The great who came to save this suffering world
> And rescue out our time's shadow, and the Law.
> Must pass beneath the yoke of grief and pain
> Heaven's riches they bring, their sufferings count the price
> Now is the debt paid, wiped of the original score ...
> The creator bears the law of pains and death;
> A retribution smites the incarnate God.

Swami Vivekananda, therefore, said that suffering is the lot of the world's best and the bravest. He said that those who wish to change the world will have to run between ecstasy and misery. He went on further to say that there can be bliss in torture too.

He rejoiced in his sufferings considering it as a supreme sacrifice. This philosophical postulation is poetically sung by Tagore as, "at every foot step of yours, will not the harp of the road break out in sweet music of pain."

He further explains suffering as being another form of grace. This he describes as,

"When I must punish him, he becomes all the more
a part of my being.
When I cause his tears to come my heart weeps with
him.
I alone have a right to blame and punish for he only
may Chastise who loves."

There is another dimension which explains the suffering in a different context. It is common that people pray particularly when undergoing pain. During lifetime a constant pursuit, a definite purpose, is to seek union with Him. Pain can thus be a message. This is poignantly portrayed through the character of Queen Kunti in *Mahabharata*. Throughout her life she had gone through trials and turmoil. However, these adversities brought Lord Krishna in close proximity to her and her family. Krishna had taught that the non-permanent nature of heat and cold is identical with happiness and distress. They come and go like winter and summer seasons. He has taught them to transcend the sense perceptions. After the war is over and Krishna is about to depart, she asks him to bestow them with calamities once again. This would ensure his arrival once more. And being with Him is the ultimate bliss.

The Indian literature is full of such stories. They highlight the merit of undergoing suffering voluntarily through an austere way of life. They also extol the virtue of giving away material possessions to satisfy the requirements of the needy. There is a story of King Rantidev. He goes on giving away his possessions. This leads him to go without food for days together. Finally, he offers the last quantity of water that he had, knowing full well that this may cause him to die. The king explains this. He would not pray to God for perfection in yoga nor for salvation. He would wish to stay amongst his fellow men and suffer all distresses on their behalf so that they may be free from suffering.

In modern times it may be interesting to note that the story almost compares with that of Tolstoy. It has been frequently debated as to whether Tolstoy really contributed anything to alleviate poverty by giving away all his possession or he added one more desolate and destitute in the world. Compared to the enormity of the suffering in the world, of what avail would be an individual's effort?

This can be best illustrated by a joke. An ant and an elephant were friends. They were going for a walk through the forest. On the way the elephant said that he was afraid since they spotted a tiger. The ant advised him to hide behind her. Compassion, when contrasted with the colossal suffering, compares most aptly with the kind feelings of the ant.

While it is fundamentally a noble quality in human relationships, without the building light of Pragnya it is helpless and powerless. Conversely compassion would arise naturally in the heart of those whose Pragnya is well-established and clear. Pragnya is man's natural attribute by which it is his fundamental right and duty to explore the mysterious realms of super consciousness.

Compassion thus adds an invaluable dimension to the human relationships whereby solace can act as an harbinger of hope, respite and retribution. However, the clarity of Pragnya of the people compelled by compassion is of paramount importance. While one Tolstoy distributing his total wealth may have added to the existing suffering through hurting his wife, his family and himself, collective actions without clarity of Pragnya at the social and political level can create calamity.

The situation in Afghanistan in August 2021 is a good illustration.

Communism, had some of the noblest and the loftiest ideas to achieve. The inspiring force was the compassion for the down-trodden. Through the contorted convulsions of a contrived methodology communism has brought havoc for half of mankind for almost a century. It will be appropriate at this juncture to illustrate the point with the conversation that transpired between Stalin and Radhakrishnan. Stalin did not grant any interview to Mrs. Pandit to present her credentials as Indian ambassador. Nehru had to, therefore, recall his sister back and replace her by Radhakrishnan. He has the audience promptly. However, he was taunted by Stalin by saying that he had no use for the philosophical wisdom except for the vision of that Indian sage who saw the image of God in the face of hungry stomachs of the exploited and the downtrodden."

Radhakrishnan's reply is relevant for all times to come. He had replied, "while hunger and the physical needs have to be primarily looked after, the quest for spirituality is the everlasting need for mankind." As a climax, suffering has been utilised as a means to self-realisation through the elaborate system of Hatha Yoga. While dwelling over practices is beyond the discussion here, the point can best be illustrated through a parable. Lord Shankara is pleased with the devotee Narsinh Mehta on account of his dedication. When offered a blessing he asked to witness the divine dance of Lord Krishna. The consort of Lord Krishna is stunned to see a human being present at the celestial event. The devotee is enthralled by the exotic experience.

He is holding a torch in his hand. But he is oblivious of the flame which has now started burning his hand. In the effulgent light of the burning flesh, the devotee is face to face with the divine. The suffering is not only of no consequence to him; he is not even aware of it. On the other hand, the radiant light provides some solutions to the trivial problems of the Krishna consort.

A fable in the Sufi literature compares well with the above parable. Mansur was a Sufi saint who had god-realisation. Thereafter he started proclaiming that he is one with God; so he is God. According to the Islamic teaching, this was blasphemy.

He was stoned. As the blood started dripping from his wounds, every drop of it proclaimed. "I am God."

People thought this to be satanic black magic and cut away his hands. Ignoring the intense pain, Mansur was seen wiping his forearms with the pouring blood. When asked what he was doing, the answer was that since he is now going to offer his final prayers, he was washing in preparation. Stunned by such fortitude and fearful of satan, people burnt his body.

Thereupon every particle of the ash started exclaiming. "I am God." When the weird remains were thrown to the sea, the ocean responded the same way.

Indian tradition thus lays great emphasis on a lifestyle of austerity and charity, at times verging on frugality. It enjoins upon all a duty to be compassionate. Interestingly enough, in the process, it is advised to act with detachment since physical self, in the end, is not the ultimate reality.

As people change old clothes and don the new, worn out body will be cast away for the new one. Therefore, render help to the extent that it may be feasible, without getting stuck in the quagmire of sentimentality. That which cannot be cured must be endured and one which is a matter of past may best be glossed over without grief. This postulate finds expression in the poetry of Khalil Gibran as:

> "The moving finger writes and having writ, moves on,
> Nor all thy tears or thy piety can erase a word of it."

This concept has been the basis of accepting passive euthanasia. A noted example is that of Vinoba Bhave. When he grew invalid, he gave up food and water.

The suffering may, thus, have some design in the holistic framework. Or is such a concept only a projection of the philosophers? Viewed from the pragmatic point of the vast majority of common man, a hungry man is interested in bread, a suffering person wants relief.

I shall, therefore, conclude by quoting the lucid and poetic description of human situation by Bertrand Russell. "United with his fellow man by the strongest of all ties, the tie of common doom, the free man finds that a new vision is with him always, shedding over every daily task the light of love. The life of Man is a long march through the night, surrounded by invisible foes, tortured by weariness and pain, towards a goal few can reach and where none may carry long.

One by one as they march, our comrades vanish from our sight, sieged by thin silent orders of Omnipotent death. Very brief is the time in which we can help them ... be it ours to shed sunshine on their path, to brighten their sorrows by the balm of sympathy, to give them the pure joy of a never tiring affection.. Let us remember that they are fellow sufferers in darkness, actors in the same tragedy with ourselves. Be it ours to feel that where they suffered, where they failed, no need of ours be the cause but whenever a spark of divine fire kindled in their hearts, we were ready with encouragement, with sympathy, with brave words in which high courage glowed. No culture will ever advise about deliberately increasing suffering or hunger. On the contrary, compassion is the common meeting point of all cultures. It is a basis on which we can attempt to build a common intercultural, international, ethical code.

Thus, witnessing the pain as a result of suffering may be one of the tools to clarify Pragnya. It generates compassion. It guides one to empathy that provides solace to both; the sufferer and the empathizer. However, compassion without a power to change the circumstances is like a wailing widowed woman. Empowerment with certain and sure means can help but without wisdom, such power also is like a blind man, waging his sword in a dark room. Hope remains, that finally wisdom shall prevail.

5
Creativity a Privilege of All

A Genius is Born—As Born Genius

Creativity has been widely researched by diverse disciplines such as anthropology, psychology, philosophy, physics, genetics, medicine etc. While we examine the concept holistically, mankind has been a witness to giant sized geniuses belonging to diverse disciplines; the benefits derived from their inventive work have provided a foundation for further building blocks of invention as well. We are dealing with normal human subjects. Creativity since time immemorial is considered to be a mystic process. The poets have found themselves to be dictated by somebody so as to create elegant poetry. Aldous Huxley postulated that there are vibes all around the brain. The insulation provided by the skull and the membranes is to protect brain getting jarred with enormity of the vibrations! Poets and philosophers share the exclusive privilege to dare speculate where no one else can even dare to dream! Most people are satisfied living a normal, well-organized life. Why would a select few—may be selected by nature as a distinctive persona, have been leading a different course of life, rather than opting for ease and comfort. The probable answer lies in the fact that they would have had a very large Pragnya quotient.

Foregoing chapters have explained about the concept of Pragnya. Indian tradition since time immemorial has extolled its virtue. But, it is of significance to note that the virtue is not described as an exclusive privilege of only a few. A misconception seems to have creeped into the description of this quality. It came to be understood that because of its sublimity, there might be something mysterious about such individuals. They came to be understood as the highly privileged children of Mother Nature. This may indeed be true provided that such a privilege is truly exceptional. Let us elaborate:

We derive empirical evidence from mathematicians Ramanujan and Shakuntaladevi. We also include two physicists, Einstein and Dirac. Einstein and Dirac, both of them received the Nobel Prize more than once.

- Ramanujan must have been the most favored child of Nature and yet not born in favorable circumstances of a supporting family. His childhood has witnessed several tragedies including death of 3 siblings and he himself suffered from the dreaded disease, smallpox. Until 10, he could not even enroll at a government funded primary school for long. His first introduction to mathematics was at the age of 10.

His school education proved him to be a distinctive student since he mastered advanced trigonometry by the age of 13 while discovering sophisticated theorems on his own. He completed mathematical exams in half the allotted time and showed familiarity with geometry and infinite series. By age 15 in 1902, he developed his own methods to solve the quartic, an advanced method of calculation. In subsequent years, he moved far ahead of the formal education till he was spotted by a Cambridge mathematician, Gilbert Walker. His work was shown earlier to a few mathematicians at the University College of London. They considered the work either a fraud or unbelievable. The worship of the value by Cambridge mathematicians proved to be a boon for Ramanujan.

Prof. Walker succeeded in recommending him to be granted a research scholarship of Rs. 75 per month at University of Madras for two years. During this period, he contributed several research papers to the *Journal of the Indian Mathematical Society.*

In a shortwhile, he received an invitation from Prof. Walker to be at Cambridge University. There is an interesting story that will serve as an interlude to advancements in mathematics by Ramanujan. His family had served at a few temples in South India. Ramanujan's mother had told him several puranic stories. This served as a link for Ramanujan to derive inspiration from a deity! There was a temple on a hill situated at Namakkal. When Ramanujan was questioned as to what is the process that he deploys for solving mathematical problems, unresolved so far, he maintained that Devi of Namakkal comes in his dreams and she provides the solutions!

Hardy and Ramanujan had highly contrasting personalities. Hardy was an atheist and an apostle of proof and mathematical rigor, whereas Ramanujan was a deeply religious man who relied very strongly on his intuitions and insights. Ramanujan died prematurely in 1920 in India. This was the time before mathematics was yet to progress to the highest degree of truth with empirical evidence, though hypotheses could be arrived at with intuition. But they would not be considered a proven science.

- Shakuntaladevi became a showcase model of Indian mathematics as a prodigy. She was thought to be a born genius. She could calculate without the help of pen, pencil or blackboard and arrive at a solution within a few seconds. She drew large audiences who paid fees to listen to her talk. She ascribed part of her methodology as derived from Vedic mathematics. Part of Vedic mathematics is now published as books but does not need to be resorted to in this age of calculators and computers.

- Albert Einstein and Paul Dirac in a chronological time scale can still be considered as prodigies during their lifespan. Science progressed at amazing speeds. When Einstein decided to permanently locate himself in the United States, in preference to Israel, several universities offered him positions and vied with each other raising not only the opportunities to conduct research but wages as well.

These are the stories of yesteryears. Mother Nature will continue to contribute to creating a genius, but the timetable is not available as to when it will occur nor can the process exactly be known.

What is precisely known today is that the population on earth has grown far beyond geometrical progression, and so has the availability of resources for higher education. Leaving less developed countries aside, the mass of the highly intelligent with prolific diverse skills has increased so much that the cutting point for the call at an interview may be as high as 100 percent by eligibility criteria. This has generated a perverse situation. Let us elucidate this further.

In contrast, there are several instances whereby geniuses happen to be a product of the circumstances. Of course, they will need high IQ and their Pragnya quotient may also, therefore, be high. But, their prize winning accomplishments are surely because of chance as to how they happen to be at one of the best institutions and so on. We illustrate with only one instance that will suffice to prove the point.

Intelligence quotient is judged to be normal when it varies between 90-110. People in this range would be suitable to carry on the roles that they happen to achieve. Say, at an interview. Eligibility criteria will be so structured. Additionally, selection of a candidate at an interview is seemingly designed so as to appear to be truly democratic. Shortlisting is mandated by the exigencies of the metrics of the recruiting institutions. Leaving aside the fallacies in the process by personal equations of the interviewer etc. even if it was a true judgment of the most suitable, the suitability pertains to the available candidates for choice. That would mean that with limited number of availability of positions, some eligible, highly deserving candidates will not be able to avail the opportunity to progress their work with a creative intent at a prestigious institution. Such adverse situations that can only be converted into opportunities are indeed rare; maybe available only to a genius. It has occurred in case of Har Gobind Khorana. He received the Nobel Prize for his research on genetics and role of nucleotides in protein synthesis. Khorana had applied for a post of assistant professor at Panjab University. He was denied and had to leave for the USA!

In contrast, Anand Bhushan Khorana succeeded in getting the post of assistant professor of Psychiatry in Gujarat. We saw signs of a fertile genius in him. Yet, he could not manage to survive in the hierarchy of government service and resigned!!

We have seen how the virtue that may be compositely called Pragnya now onwards manifests in most normal human beings and have also studied fluctuations in Pragnya. We shall simply catalogue two other such occurrences that we have discussed earlier, viz. Arthur Koestler and others.

While some exceptional cases like the enigma as to how even a schizophrenic John Nash can win a Nobel Prize remain unsolved, we are proceeding now to ascertain whether there is any special quality of Pragnya to the inventors of various kinds.

We have already discussed Charak's postulates. Modern times have enlarged our understanding of Pragnya to include personality types based on 'Sattva', 'Rajas' and 'Tamas'. How they influence the motivations for action is described by Gitanjali

Roy as Pragnya Quotient (Ch. 6: Psychological Perspective of Pragnya).

Let us first examine the creative process of invention.

It is taken for granted that Pragnya quotient is an intrinsic attribute of all normal human beings, even if they were to differ in judgment, they would be considered normal. One of the best empirical evidence of the above is differing judgments by the Justices of Supreme Courts across the world!

This is how a normal life goes on in society at various normative levels. Creativity is perceived with awe, surprise and wonder. It is an 'Aha!' experience. The viewer also feels how it could have ever happened! The surprise surmounts to even astonishment so that one is left spellbound. Archimedes ran naked through the streets to report to a tyrannical king as to how he has solved a difficult puzzle about the gold in the crown. It is also documented that Kekule's dream experience was instrumental in discovery of the benzene ring. Taking the analogy of the process to recent times, let us review how Watson and Crick deciphered the helical structure of the DNA molecule. They were jointly awarded the 1962 Nobel Prize in Physiology or Medicine "for their discoveries concerning the molecular structure of nucleic acids and its significance for information transfer in living materials."

They worked for several years to decipher and answer two questions. One was, how does life begin and the other was, how does consciousness manifest in inert substances? They found the second question far too difficult (and yet not resolved) and focused to find the beginning of life. They established that DNA—Deoxyribonucleic Acid is the primary molecule that has a property to replicate itself. That was the beginning of life.

The structure of the molecule DNA was arrived at with a sudden insight by Watson. After working late at night, he put out a random design of the sequences of amino acids that may constitute the molecule DNA. He got up late. Suddenly, when he glanced on the tabletop, he thought with subliminal illumination, he had arrived at the correct amino acid sequence. There was an exalted feeling of elation for Watson and Crick both. They announced it by climbing a table in a pub! (Why would they have chosen a pub and a tabletop to announce their discovery? Any media person in the present times or even then would gladly put it on a frontpage. Putting it with a tongue in cheek mode, they may have taken too much to drink!)

However, present times do not need this kind of sudden appearance of insight or metaphoric mystic dreams to discover creative events. Intuitive insights may still be available to some privileged people. How the privilege will accrue to any individual will become an undemocratic question. Let it be left to discussion between various political thinkers. We restrict ourselves to a large mass of humanity. Thus creativity needs to be understood with a different yardstick.

It may, therefore, happen that even the privileged few with a high Pragnya quotient may not be discerniable in the society. They provide the metrics of wisdom to a sustainable environment and enduring society.

We postulate that while a normal Pragnya quotient, say at about 100, may be the attribute of most human beings, there could be a normal range of variation. A brilliant intellectual would have an IQ of 140+. This person with a psychometric assessment of Pragnya, is likely to generate a Pragnya quotient more than that of the average. Such persons may amount to 5 per cent of humanity. Even then, whether they write a single line of poetry or sketch a pencil drawing or end up with inventions in a scientific discipline will be a matter of chance. It takes a seed, fertile soil and a generous environment for the crop to flourish. Let us look at the environment that may support creativity. We have elucidated that suffering provides a motherground to creativity in previous chapters (Chapter 4: Deep Distress has Humanized my Soul).

Here, we enlarge the concept with empirical evidence from prehistoric times.

The genesis of *Ramayana*, a great work of art, apart from being a significant religious text, points to an interesting origin. Before the actual composition of the work, it is said that Sage Valmiki was at a loss as to how to begin the epic. So when he was groping, struggling, experiencing the pangs and throes of creativity, it so happened that he saw a female krauncha (stork) bird distraught with grief, weeping and wailing. The cause of its sorrow was occasioned by the sudden death of its partner under tragic circumstances. A cruel hunter had shot down the male krauncha bird when it was making love to its beloved. As a consequence the widowed female bird started lamenting over the death of its dear one.

The compassionate sage was so deeply moved on seeing the miserable plight of the poor female bird that he involuntarily burst into song: "Ma nishada. . ."(translates as whatever you may do, but don't do that) which itself became the starting point (the Mangala-shloka) of the *Ramayana*. Shoka (grief) was transformed into shloka (song) which explains why pathos or karuna rasa is the dominant emotion of the *Ramayana*. The heart-rending scene that Sage Valmiki had witnessed was such that he was stirred to his depths and not being able to contain all that emotion, he spontaneously broke into a song. This is a classic case of transmuting one's personal sorrow through an act of creativity.

This kind of experience is ubiquitous, all over the world; across cultures and religions. Even today, the memory of Jesus Christ being crucified with rivers of blood flowing through each wound generates compassionate kindness for most Catholics.

A derivation with psychoanalysis is thus derived that inten
grieving also strikes like a lightning that goes into th
depths that may amount to a numerous myriad
memory deeply buried in the farthest depths

mind. The fountain of creativity so discovered contains variable virtues of compassion, kindness, sharing and forgiveness.

Real life empirical evidence far apart from the epic occurs everyday in most of the houses all over the world. That is the love of a mother. Love is many a splendored thing. Though Freudian psychoanalysts have also considered the motivation of some kind of self-gratification in service of ego to almost all love relationships, they have conceded that love of a mother for an offspring is a singular exception. There is a continuous insurmountable urge to give and to my dear child take even my heart!

This permanent bonding to unconditional giving arises from the pangs of labor pains that an expectant mother has to undergo for several hours. Hearing the first cry of a newborn baby is enough of a joy to overcome the labor pains. This is well-documented in neuroscience as well. When two extremes of opposite sensations try to capture the attention in the brain, the dominant one prevails to the exclusion altogether of the other.

It is pertinent to cite another empirical evidence of this relationship. A brilliant criminal lawyer was famous for his ability to manipulate law and the legal system so that most murderers would get acquitted. The prevalent advice in the criminal world in the province was that one need not be afraid of a death sentence so long as he could afford to hire that particular lawyer.

The mother and son lived in the same house. One day the mother came to know that a certain husband had brutally murdered his wife. Orgy of violence had splattered blood all over the place. Cries, wailing and pleading for help were heard all over the neighborhood. Yet, nobody dared to rush to help. There was no eyewitness. Next day, she told her lawyer son, "Dhiru, this murderer will come to your office today. If you handle this case, I cannot live with you!" The lawyer son was casual. He said, "Every criminal has a right for self-defense. That is the law of the land and I am doing my professional duty that provides bread to both of us."

The lawyer capitalized on a single fact that there was no eyewitness. He managed to get the murderer acquitted! Jurisprudence germinates through the foundations of human behavior. That is indeed noble. In the same vein, it is said that, but the law is an ass. It does not rely on such facts which move the heart of a mother.

The mother came to know about the brilliant success that her clever son had achieved. She told him, "If this is providing the bread in this house, I cannot have any bread, not even water in this house!" She left.

The repentant son could only win the confidence of the mother when he promised that he would not pursue the profession as a criminal lawyer any more. Mother and son were united to live in the same house. Nature rewarded the repentant to be elevated to the status of a Supreme Court justice.

The story would be forgotten soon by the people of Gujarat. But, Justice Dhirubhai Desai is remembered to have dispensed justice with kindness and mercy.

A seminal judgment by Justice Desai is being cited in the annals of the law even today. An old widowed woman who had lost her husband while serving in Indian Army was entitled to pension. She was illiterate and unable to afford legal help. She could only write a few sentences on a postcard to the Supreme Court, New Delhi. It was brought to the attention of Justice Dhirubhai Desai. He found it enough to initiate a *suo motu* proceeding against the Government of India! This time also he won, providing pension to all such women who fell in that category.

We have seen how a sudden jolt or suffering may provide a bifurcation point that leads to generation of pristine, pure Pragnya. High values to virtues such as compassion, generosity etc. have been provided since ancient times and will continue to be available to humanity for long. A few will utilize sentiments associated with them to propagate personal gains so that politicians will succeed in beguiling the innocent populace and win votes. This should not in any way diminish what is good value. However, what is past is bygone. It can serve only as a milestone or may be like a rear view mirror in a car for the historians. The empirical evidence should be such as to be lasting with the test of time as well. At the onset we may assert that creativity is a mother ground that surely and certainly yields lasting results. Thus lasting results may be a litmus test for creativity.

What is the time scale to measure for a research to be lasting? We saw in the previous chapter about Roger Sperry and how his understanding proved to be of limited utility within a few decades. Therefore, we shall surely need to give credit to whoever dares to probe a creative process. But, it appears more likely that they are like blind men in search of what is an 'elephant'. Recitation of the story will give us a pause that will be useful for further discourse.

A group of five blind men heard that an elephant had been brought to the town, but none of them had seen an elephant before. They were curious, how an elephant would appear. They could only judge by touching since they did not have eyesight. So, they sought it out, and when they found it they touched different parts. The first person touched the trunk and said, "This being is like a thick snake". To the other blind man whose hand reached its ear, it seemed like a kind of fan. For another person, whose hand was upon its leg, the elephant was like a pillar, a tree-trunk. The blind man who placed his hand upon its side said the elephant "is a wall". Another who felt its tail described it as a rope.

We will give credit to the veracity of each blind man. They could only describe what they had felt. All of them are true. But, taken as a whole, they have not understood what it means to be an elephant.

We take a review of what so far has been researched either with elegant logic or with brilliant mathematics or by other scientific disciplines.

Some researchers have thought that the creative process works like Janusian thinking, which comes from the Roman God Janus who has two faces. One facing the front, and the other facing the back. This has been utilized even while working on rewriting this manuscript with a reVision after more than 30 years. If a work is so arduous, so as to need such a long time for reflection, creativity needed not only the flash, the inspiration, the peak experience; but also needed hard work, long training, unrelenting criticism, and perfectionist standards highlighting the role of consciousness in streamlining the unconscious perceptions that have surfaced.

Poets have abdicated personal responsibility in service of humility. They said that there was a 'divine source' and simply they transcribed. On the contrary, the process was said to be engineered by a 'Ghost in the Machine'[1]. This may have been a currency for 50 years and more before. Today not even school children are enamored to read stories about Gods and divinity. In the similar vein, ghosts are relegated into the minds of the superstitious and comparison of the mind to a machine is also redundant. As toys in the palm of their hand, children play with what would have been compared to a supercomputer a few decades ago. Information pool on the earth is said to be doubling within 7 years; that was pre-computer age. Now it happens so in 13 months! Yet, there is much rapid access with computers and encyclopedias have become redundant. But, it has emerged that supercomputers of today do work faster than the brain. The innovations have percolated in all the disciplines; even in stock market and broking houses that has earned international fame, namely Morgan Stanley and Templeton. They have not studied philosophy or mathematics. Yet, they come to amass a large fortune. Templeton Foundation has divested funds for creative activities.

It might be considered mundane by philosophers to discuss trade and commerce. However, considering all empirical evidences as good evidence, we dare not shun away. Some manipulations in the stock market would have needed high intelligence that cannot be said to be entirely a prerogative for highly educated or wise men.

Indian stock market witnessed such a phenomenal success in a broker, namely Harshad Mehta. He was only a matriculate. He beguiled and manipulated several bankers and broking houses.

Another empirical evidence is Ketan Parekh. He manipulated only 10 scripts that came to be known as K-P Scripts. He was successful in taking the scripts to superlative highs, certainly not with any accounting methods but mere manipulation.

Indian stock market has witnessed several such masterly manipulations that a freak saying has come into vogue; 'Usually when happy, a dog wags its tail. When the tail wags the dog, stock markets are happy!'

We are not discussing the morals of such manipulations. If the Pragnya of such people was to be rooted in noble qualities such as compassion, concern for public welfare, it is likely that they would not have finally been doomed.

We take into review yet another field. Sports and athletics would appear far distant from what may be a psychic component Pragnya would account for. It takes only a little reflection to understand how a tennis player will score several grand slams or a particular football player will score maximum goals and so on. Before scoring his first championship trophy, a tennis player would have had several years of training; with a seasoned senior player. Such rigorous, long standing apprenticeship would have provided the player with experience as to what speed a tennis ball would travel when hit with a certain force. He would be further equipped that what distance the ball must not travel so as to drop just within a few inches of the border line. These calculations have to be done on the spur of the moment. Judging the space as measurements of distance would mean that the right side of the brain provides the necessary input. Calculation of the speed and the force applied to the ball would involve mathematics. This may seem to be contributed by the left side of the brain. Obviously a tennis player has no concern with this kind of analysis. His persistent perseverance with long hours of training has equipped him with all the information that may be accounted for as a whole brain function. Similar analogy may be applied to a football champion as to what degree his knee should be bent and to hit with what force etc. He will also be using his whole brain.

Creative activity has thus expanded to a panoramic expanse that will include deployment of computers to access information far and wide. Computation has pierced deep down so that data that would have been stored into terabytes amounting to x number can also be retrieved in a few seconds.

Thus, an individual human brain has an access to a wide, wide resource pool of knowledge that has been accumulated through the efforts of highly intelligent, innumerable human brains! This has percolated far and wide into various systems, maybe accounting, architecture and molecular biology! For expanding the available pool of information in physiology and medicine, an altogether new discipline, namely bioinformatics has come into being. With the medium of this system, computer software establishes linkages, so that experiments involving lengthy procedures and high expenses can be bypassed. Not only what is proven is accessed but also a hypothesis can be generated.[2]

We cite empirical evidence from bioinformatics. Our innovative research with use of stem cells also derived postulation of a hypothesis through bioinformatics.[3]

A different state of awareness, Turya the fourth state, may be a generic ground. However, the invention so conceptualized in this state as symbols will need translations into a language that can convey the meaning. We have seen Albert Einstein arrive at his inventions in a dream state that seems akin to what is described as Turya. Yet, a mathematician that he was, he would translate his symbols to convey meaning through an equation. Impressionist painters including Pablo Picasso visualized abstract forms. They so painted as to convey an aesthetic meaning to the viewers and so on.

Whether such a creative invention is indeed a lasting invention needs reality testing. This is a time tested model for approval across various fields. Initially, it involves self reflection, peer validation, and critical evaluation. Final proof may be provided by a large number of reviewers. The litmus test would be a translation to a product of public utility at affordable prices!

We have seen that such a large critical value may prove even Pablo Picasso to be wrong in judging his paintings.

Logical reasoning is generally applied to judge creativity of an invention. It must be entirely novel thinking in progression of a process or may be in making a novel product. Only statements verifiable through direct observation or logical proof are meaningful in terms of conveying truth value, information or factual content. This also has a limit case as far as true value of creativity is concerned. Let us cite empirical evidences:

1. A brilliant lawyer went on arguing a case in favour of his client. Midway through, he was passed a chit by his assistant, 'Sir, you are arguing for our opponents. The case will go in their favour!'

The lawyer said to the court, "Sir, this is what my opponents will argue before you. Now, I shall take each and every point and quash it verbatim!" He destroyed his own logical arguments so as to win the case!

2. Stephen Hawking has contributed immensely, though crippled in a wheelchair bound state. Later in his life, he could hardly speak intelligent language.

He has written that utilizing Newtonian physics, he can prove that every miniscule occurrence on planet Earth was predetermined by an event.

Conversely, he said he can as well prove that any occurrence in the universe is a chance happening. This will be based on quantum physics.

Thus let us accept a limit case to logical positivism as well. As far as it is verifiable with empirical evidence, a creative invention may indeed be true till such a time that further inventions negate this one.

Karl Popper, a philosopher investigating scientific inventions has concluded that scientific inventions progress by negating the previous inventions! It is easy to prove Karl Popper either as true or false with logical positivism.

Such narration may tantamount to eulogizing the previous investigators. The list can prolong to an indefinite length. It is pertinent that every investigator is correct to the extent as to what he might have examined; such as a leg, or an ear, or a trunk of the elephant. We need to examine mathematicians' viewpoints since mathematics is a perfect science.

This is indeed so and can easily be deciphered that numerical value of a digit conveys one and the only one meaning such as 1 is equal to one, 2 is equal to two and so on. This is true even for fractals. Fractals can be easily understood with an example:

It is illustrated by the simple division of a straight line into a triangle. That can further be extended to more triangles; the angles of the triangle may vary until it generates a curvature. Even a small fragment of the curvature can give an image of a straight line; that was a motherground to generate a triangle!

Symbolism with fractals is also seen in a pictorial form of creation of sea waves. As we see the tidal waves approaching the sea shore, gathering more and more force with increasing tidal force, they keep on creating a form of a 'seahorse' (Fig. 5.1). That is known as the Mandelbrot set.

Fig. 5.1: Partial view of the Mandelbrot set

The seahorse "body" is composed of 25 "spokes" consisting of two groups of 12 "spokes" each and one "spoke" connecting to the main cardioid. These two groups can be attributed by some kind of metamorphosis to the two "fingers" of the "upper hand" of the Mandelbrot set; therefore, the number of "spokes" increases from one "seahorse" to the next by 2.

A mathematician will view this in the form of an algorithm. Algorithms in mathematics are a progression with time sequence progressing to a finite or infinite state. Psychologically the process in the brain is similar to creation of a pattern with a sequence of 'seahorses'. It occurs at subliminal, better called now as the unconscious level of the mind. Here an intellectual and creative person keeps on repeating, revising, recapitulating with verification, revalidation and even discarding as not true. Let us illustrate this in the language of numericals. They are classified as recursive and non-recursive.

Recursive—Whereby the same number can be arrived at by multiplication/division.

Non-recursive—Where the same number cannot be so arrived at. The best illustration of this is 22/7 or π. One can keep on repeating the division that can proceed to infinity. But, the division cannot be completed. Therefore, there is no recurrence available. Carrying the analogy to psychological process of creative invention, when a theorem drives to a definite point, may be drafted in a mathematical formula, so as to arrive at a conclusion, creative process may end up with 'Eureka!', or in the language of Happy Molecules as 'Aha!' experience. Alternatively after carrying the mental process several times over and over again, it keeps on generating non-recursive numbers. The inventor will have to conclude that his efforts have been futile and are in vain.

Herein lies a probable transformation in a creative stage. When Einstein describes his creative interplay as a dialogue between symbols, he would thus utilize fractals to arrive at a formula such as $E = mc^2$. This formula and such other formulae arrived at by physicists are also symbolically fractals: that generates numerous derivations and so on.

Let us illustrate with one more empirical evidence from mathematics:

> One more mathematical illustration is zero. Zero multiplied by zero is zero. Zero divided by zero is also zero. Philosophically the concept of a whole also is that which incorporates the wholeness of the original. Material illustration of wholeness is, say, gold. When subdivided up to the atomic scale, it remains gold. Several abstractions also illustrate wholeness, such as the test of a grain of sugar which will retain the same sweetness.

Based on all above it is pertinent to describe the creative process of invention as follows:

> The stages of creativity are Preparation, Incubation, Verification and Peak experience. Creativity meant establishing the underlying association or a link amongst different entities which might take on the form of 1. Serendipity—hitting at an answer by chance or accident. 2. Similarity—associative elements appearing in the form of contiguity, pattern or rhyme. 3. Mediation—different elements are associated at the symbolic level, and scientists are supposed to belong to this group.

The process of creativity may be illustrated with the following figure:

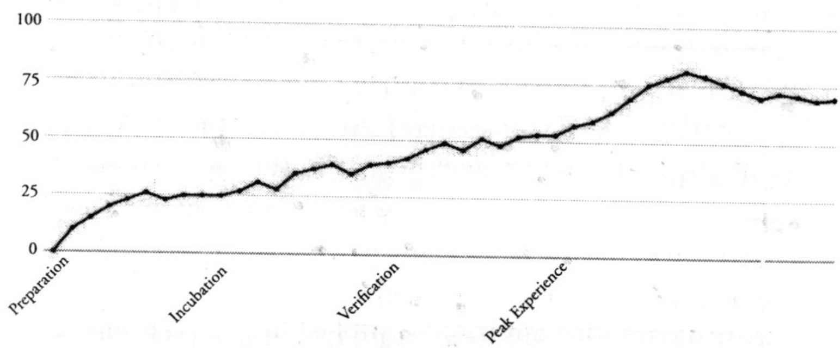

Fig. 5.2: Process of Creativity

Based on the discussion above, we may arrive at the following surmise:

- Rishi Charak was on a sound foundation when he coined the axiom, '*Dhi, Dhruti and Smruti Iti Pragnya*'. Translated as intellect, persistence and patience, and memory taken together constitutes (a composite quality of personality) Pragnya. This led to the foundation for Indian science of long life and preventive health, viz. Ayurveda. The science did provide sound clues to understand the etiology of certain mental disorders. However, defining Pragnya with only the quoted three determinants will still leave a lacunae.

Present study aims at arriving at 21st century understanding. Obviously times have changed from Charak's era. Taking recourse to Indian idiom only, it will be pertinent now that personality profile of the individual may also be added to adjudge the measurement of Pragnya quotient. The qualities of personality traits based on *Sattva, Rajas* and *Tamas* are well catalogued in Ayurveda.

Therefore, Pragnya quotient will be arrived at by incorporating the personality profiles as well. In consonance with modern times, psychologists will also apply mathematical scales to Pragnya quotient.

- In normal individuals also, Pragnya undulates.

It is a fundamental attribution for every individual to experience happiness—joy. Molecules of happiness have been identified.

Down gradation of Pragnya may occur when any kind of neurosis is resorted in service of ego. Shining mirror of Pragnya would not reflect light in these situations.

- Eclipse of Pragnya is also seen in what otherwise might seem to be normal individuals. The eclipse may pass away by itself.

Meditation by whatsoever name may provide an easy and early return to normalcy from the eclipse.

- Various noble qualities may be considered as attributes of *Sattva guna.* Though essentially spiritual, they permeate the very core of societal structures across the hemispheres.

However, taken in isolation, they have only little to contribute to Pragnya.

A democratic societal structure prevalent as current currency in modern civilization has provided everyone with an opportunity to be in a position of power. Spiritual virtues may illuminate but it is obvious that power is a must in order to execute.

- In the situation of various kinds that amount to upsurge of happiness and downgradation of various intellectual faculties, a powerful person is truly vulnerable to misjudge. Only when he is empowered with wisdom to cope, and to surmount such vicissitudes with wisdom, he can act right.
- When faced with a bifurcation point between opposite choices, there is no litmus test available to decide between the choices. Illumination with an insight that may be generated through the medium of elegant, beautiful and lyrical poetry may be available at all times, but, would be taken recourse to by only so inclined and educated.
- There is overwhelming evidence that most people think with the whole brain.

Thus it may be justified that inventions in the 21st century may occur by people endowed with a high Pragnya quotient. It is, therefore, justified that now onwards geniuses will not be born only; they can be made out of circumstances. A person would certainly need a high Pragnya quotient but accessory situations that make the person to be at the right place and at the right time, will determine whether he qualifies to be called a genius! There is numerous empirical evidence still available. However, what is already proved as above does not need any further evidence.

Notes

1. Arthur Koestler wrote a psychophilosophical treatise titled 'Ghost in the Machine' in 1967. The title and scholastic postulations were so fanciful for Koestler to be awarded noteworthy awards.
2. D. Atkinson, S. Iannotti, M. Cozzolino, B. Vyas, K. Rossi, E. Rossi *et al.* (2010). A New Bioinformatics Paradigm for the Theory, Research, and Practice of Therapeutic Hypnosis, *American Journal of Clinical Hypnosis*, 53:1, 27-46, DOI: 10.1080/00029157.2010.10401745
3. B. Vyas, R. Vyas, A. Marathe (2020). Revisiting Melanin Metabolism with revision, *Global Journals of Science Frontier Research.*

6
Psychological Perspective of Pragnya

—Gitanjali Roy, Ph.D.[1]

Pragyanidhi, an old classmate of mine of whom I always remember as one with a traditional and mystical name. She is kind, wise, intelligent and composed person. May be names do affect personality or *vice versa*. After nearly two decades I am remembering and writing about her because I am analyzing 'Pragnya' from a psychological perspective.

Western psychology has dominated the psychological knowledge paradigm in India since early nineteenth century. It explains pragnya as an intuitive mind or intuition that people can cultivate with a set of exercises (like quizzing with blindfolds) as guided by a teacher. I find it rather incomplete as the presentation lacks any relation with personality, intelligence or any other human abilities. Those exercises are not incorrect but their explanations are limited and incomplete. So I move to the Indian Philosophy, the treasury of knowledge for a better understanding of Pragnya.

The Indian Knowledge System has numerous ancient scriptures in her bosom to nurture the minds of people for intellectual, spiritual and personal development. Pragnya has numerous meanings and mentions in scriptures like *Yogasutra*, *Charaka Samhita*, *Ayurveda* and many more.

Understanding Pragnya on Indian Psychological Front

Charaka was an ancient scholar well known for his illustrative contributions in the field of ancient medicinal science. He extended from physical to psychological understanding of human mind and body to support a holistic living and cure. He was a believer of knowledge and its comprehension by human mind on three levels—*jagrita, nidra* and *sushupti.* A person experiences knowledge at physical level through senses and at sleep level through dreams, but when he moves beyond these states his knowledge experiences shackle the physical and psychological barriers making it true or experiential knowledge, a state of *Pragnya* understanding. In other words, when mind is free from worldly ties and ready to evolve beyond tangible attributes, one experiences *Pragnya,* i.e. an unbiased understanding of knowledge and a discriminant intellect. After Charaka, I can recall verses from *Yogasutra* postulated by Maharshi Patanjali popularly known as founder of yoga. His opinion on pragnya is similar to Charaka but more elaborated. For him, pragnya emerges when person acquires a higher state of consciousness, i.e. the true sense of being or full awareness of self. Here consciousness shall not be limited to its literal meaning of being awake or aware of surroundings. It is rather a magnified sense of awareness completely based on experiential knowledge and not just physical surroundings. People become aware by gaining knowledge through books, television, social media and experience. But the knowledge based on evidences and interpretation brings pragnya as it magnifies the awareness halo.

Is Pragnya the correct knowledge or mental faculty?

Pragnya is a combination of *dhi, dhriti* and *smriti*, the Sanskrit terms meaning intellect, self-control and memory respectively. The function of *dhi* (buddhi or intellect) is to prepare a paradigm of knowledge in the human mind to make decisions, solve problems and engage in intuitive thinking.

Rational and logical thinking are also product of intellect. Triguna plays a significant role in pragnya and its components. The sattva guna qualities include patience, altruism, spiritual and intutive of their actions. Rajas guna includes being active, passionate, boastful and greedy. The tamoguna includes indolence, inertia, belief in anti-spirituality and pessimism. The true nature of intellect or dhi is sattvik dominated by Sattva guna. So the true function is virtue and justice, letting it make thinking rationale, decisions right and the mind free from any delusions or biases. When individual intakes a knowledge with a discriminant intellect, comprehend it patiently and store it in memory that knowledge evolves you to the state of *pragnya*. Human mind has the ability to use his *dhi*, intellect for refining an information to its authenticity, i.e. scrutinize the information to its fragments and identify its genuineness only to accept as a true knowledge. The other two gunas—rajas and tamas are also part of intellect but if they overpower sattva guna the interpretation of knowledge becomes clouded with falsehood and imperfections. In such a situation person begins to deviate from the path of virtue and enter the net of misinterpretations. Once the intellect acquires authentic information *dhriti* (self-control) helps to act to the wise decision taken by the dhi. Here self-control also controls the mind and its fluctuations. In our daily lives, with intellect by our side, a control over mind is either learned or acquired through various sattvik practices like meditation. Rajas and tamasguna help in making the mind more active and unstable, making it difficult to decide or stick to it. They bring our attention to sensual gratification from materialistic objects in the world.

Dhritivibrastha, or imbalance of self-control makes it impossible to let the intellect function in wisdom.

The process of mental endurance requires both *dhi*, intellect and *dhriti*, self-control. Intellect or *dhi* includes memory too from past experiences. Our memory system has three sections to process an information—the sensory memory, short-term and long-term memory and of these three only the long term memory is capable of storing events, birthdates etc. form of information. For an efficient *smriti*, memory process individual has to make a conscious investment in the processing of information from sensory to long term memory. With an intact intellect and patience, he stores and increases the capacity of the memory. From memory, when the recollection of knowledge is impaired, i.e. inability to recall is experienced it indicates derangement of smriti or smritivibrashtha.

Generally, tamasguna dominance leads to such condition as its function is to bring inertia. Person fails to make proper decisions or appropriate behavior due to incognizance, a result of tamoguna and sometime rajoguna too. These two gunas in excess can cause cognitive disturbances in individual. Sattva guna when dominates the *dhi, dhriti* comes handy making *smriti* function aptly thus aligning the person on the path of righteousness and equilibrium.When an individual finds a balance between all the three gunas, not dominated by either of the three and finds himself evolving out of them to attain pragnya. *Shrimad Bhagavad Gita* (in chapter two verse fifty-four) emphasizes that Arjun should evolve out these triguna and only then he will be an endowed person with pragnya, i.e. wise, stable and capable to experience the truth. Here, Arjun symbolizes every person and he must attain pragnya by making himself free from the effects of all the three gunas. In synchronicity, pragnya is a result of trigunateet and a harmony among *dhi, dhriti* and *smriti*; thus resulting into a superior state of *buddhi* processing knowledge. Such a superior processing is a result of interaction among the object of knowledge, senses in contact with this object and *chitta* (mind). A *pragyavant* has *dhriti, dhi* and *smriti* balanced functioning not in the moment but for a longer run. In psychological terms, a balanced person has his cognitive abilities balanced in such a manner that he makes use of his intellect to process and store relevant information for better prospects. So a balance among *triguna* (with sattva high and rajas and tamas medium to low) brings a mental equilibrium among intellect, self-control and memory.

Role of Triguna and Pragnya

Triguna has a significant role in defining the personality of people. *Sankhyakarika* and *Shrimad Bhagavad Gita* has supported the existence of this postulate: The consciousness of every human being percolates down to the interplay of trigunas. *Dhi, dhriti* and *smriti* are products of triguna. Each guna share their domination over these three factors for pragnya hence influencing the mind of people.

Intellect or *dhi* is specifically dominated by the sattva guna, hence is its primary functions being illumination, knowledge gaining and purity of mind and body. *Dhriti*, the self-control under the influence of sattva guna applies surveillance to the sanctity of the intellect. But with rajas and tamas, the person cannot have a stable *dhriti* because of the unstable mind, over influence of emotions and being focused of achieving materialistic goals.

In cognitive, behavioural and emotional processes the triguna tends to undergo an interaction and imbalance to fulfil the requirements. Environment does influence this movement but the mind has the power to handle it. Proper synchronism of triguna leads to intelligent and wise execution of knowledge resulting into evolution of manhood (from mundane to spiritual enlightenment). This successful synchronism is extended to *dhi*, *dhriti* and *smriti*. Ayurveda, *Shrimad Bhagavad Gita* and other ancient scriptures have shown the path to a faraway land of enlightenment. This can be an aspiration but most people remain far away from it, though they are capable to carry on the task that has been enjoined to their professional duties. Obviously they will have a high level of Pragnya that can be ascertained with Pragnya quotient as postulated by us.

Let us find an answer to the state of Pragnya when Trigunas are functional in variable proportions. As discussed earlier, the sattva guna precedes the proper functioning of dhi, intellect. But to find knowledge in its pure sattvik form is difficult. Because most of it are comprehensible by the dominance of sattva, rajas and tamasguna. Hence to find the correct knowledge one needs to nurture the sattva guna over the other two gunas and gradually evolve out of the sattva guna too.Trigunateet or growing out of the effects of triguna brings in pragnya where the knowledge is manifested for wisdom, intellect, self-control and memory expands the opportunity for a man to function to their fullest of threshold (towards excellence) and he frees himself from improper actions and decisions of life. The improper decision can be listed as confusion, delusion and falsehood. When the knowledge from smriti is different from the interpretation by intellect, the result is confusion or *samasya.* In case of delusion, intellect concludes that knowledge is wrong without any reason or with the momentary reason. Finally, the falsehood means when satavik (proper) or rajasic and tamasic (improper) states of knowledge are considered by the dhi, dhriti and smriti.

Understanding Pragnya with Intelligence quotient and Emotional Quotient

Pragnyaparadha and Imbalance in Triguna

Those people with impaired intellect, self-control and memory have intellectual blasphemy or pragnyaparadha.

The concept has a wide application at various societal levels. People seem to be functioning and living an apparently normal life when their Pragnya levels are low. To assess the levels of Pragnya would, therefore, be highly relevant that will provide a cybernetic autocorrective information.

The Pragnya Scale

Introduction

The triguna are ingrained personality constituents that make a man what he is, guiding him through various aspects of life. In human life, spirituality has played a pivotal role in keeping mind intact. A person who can find himself functioning harmoniously with all the three gunas and gradually not depending on their application, is called pragna. To such people, knowledge comes intuitively, experientially, as well as with discursive didactic rationality as well. For example, a doctor with pragnya will make use of her years of experience and intuitiveness to examine a pregnant woman to conclude the time and type of delivery. At the same time the doctor will also use the scientific table to correctly estimate the date of delivery. This doctor is a pragna.

This instrument identifies the pragna quotient. But for a holistic personality assessment, I suggest you must undergo Intelligence test and Emotional test for IQ and EQ for academic purposes. High scores on both these tests shall be collated with the following pragna inventory to assess the pragna quotient of individual.

Instructions

For each statement, please mark one answer from the suggested options on the right side (strongly agree to strongly disagree). No statement or answer is right or wrong so you are requested to attend all the statements honestly.

Thank you.

Sl. No.	Question	Strongly Disagree -1	Disagree -2	Neutral -3	Agree -4	Strongly Agree -5
1	I believe I have a logical and rational mind that makes realistic decisions.					
2	I believe I have strong motivation towards my goal.					
3	I am being told by my family and friends that I am a practical person when it comes to decision-making.					
4	I have to be loud while making my family and friends follow my decision. I have complexity in solving any problems at work or home.					
5	I believe in my intuitions about outcome of certain tasks.					
6	I see myself as an analytical or a logical thinker.					
7	I critically analyze every aspect of my work, decisions and actions.					
8	I trust my intuitions or immediate feelings about people.					
9	I believe that with people I cannot make an immediate judgement.					
10	I am not comfortable in those situations where I have a conflict between my feelings and the visible evidences either about a person or event.					

(*Contd.*)

Sl. No.	Question	Strongly Disagree -1	Disagree -2	Neutral -3	Agree -4	Strongly Agree -5
11	I find my reasoning ability challenged under pressure (work or family pressure).					
12	I feel satisfied when I have opportunity to think deep and for a long time.					
13	I depend on my intuitions to solve problems.					
14	I indulge in various pleasurable activities (such as food, drinks, sex etc.) as they free my mind from stress.					
15	I am alert and conscious about my actions (such as reading, chatting with people etc.).					
16	I tend to over-indulge in pleasurable activities (such as food, drinks, sex etc.) as they give me immense satisfaction.					
17	I use help from professionals in case of difficulty.					
18	I do not believe that any one can help me so I keep my problems to myself.					
19	I engage in deep thinking because it makes me reason mine or others actions.					
20	Activities like thinking, intuitive engagement, observing are not enjoyable by me.					

(*Contd.*)

Sl. No.	Question	Strongly Disagree -1	Disagree -2	Neutral -3	Agree -4	Strongly Agree -5
21	My way of problem solving is careful analysis of each aspect of the problem, intuitive thinking, reach out for professional help (if required) and then concluding.					
22	For solving any problems I prefer to use my past experiences and then wait for the results.					
23	I do not find myself comfortable in a situation that requires problem solving.					
24	I have a clear and proper explanation for my decisions.					
25	I do not believe in giving any explanations to my decisions.					
26	When compared to my friends or family or collegues, I use logic and analysis to figure out things in my life.					
27	I rely on my intuitions while trusting people.					
28	I trust people based on facts and past experiences (either with them or not).					
29	I use my knowledge and experience in guiding my feelings to make decisions.					

(*Contd.*)

Sl. No.	Question	Strongly Disagree -1	Disagree -2	Neutral -3	Agree -4	Strongly Agree -5
30	For comprehending my environment, I rely on my knowledge, experience and feelings.					
31	I can feel, but cannot explain when a person is correct or incorrect.					
32	I find learning new things interesting.					
33	I engage in learning new information or learning new things.					
34	I engage in intellectual competitions.					
35	I engage in abstract thinking.					
36	I argue my way out of any conversation with friends, colleagues or seniors.					
37	I am told that my nature is argumentative than discussion based.					
38	I know certain answers without knowing the reason behind it.					
39	I can reach to certain decisions without knowing how I reached there.					
40	I find it easy to solve problems where deep thinking is needed.					

(*Contd.*)

Sl. No.	Question	Strongly Disagree -1	Disagree -2	Neutral -3	Agree -4	Strongly Agree -5
41	I am enchanted by the beauty of various fame, charms and belongings in my life.					
42	I am able to let go any negative thoughts about any person from past or present.					
43	I remember every bad incidence from past to take revenge in future.					
44	I trust people based on their financial background and opinion of others about them.					
45	I avoid unpleasant stimulus as much as possible by any possible means.					
46	I accept pain and pleasure situations with an open mind.					
47	I react the moment I feel someone attacks me with their words or attitude.					
48	I manage my impulses to avoid conflicts with others.					
49	I am not hesitant in opening a fight to prove my point.					
50	I have problem trusting my authorities/seniors at work.					
51	I have problem trusting my elders at home/family.					
52	I face internal conflict that I am unable to resolve myself.					

(*Contd.*)

Sl. No.	Question	Strongly Disagree -1	Disagree -2	Neutral -3	Agree -4	Strongly Agree -5
53	I find a reason or a person to blame for my internal conflicts.					
54	I have learned that in this society I have to play by games (like lying, gossiping, cheating) in order to survive.					
55	I feel anxious, sense of losing my identity in workspace.					
56	I feel anxious, sense of losing my identity in home/family functions.					
57	I believe that people are out to get me whether at work or home.					
58	I do not believe in threatening facts like death of someone close or lose of expensive item.					
59	People who know me well have mentioned to me that I hide my true feelings by acting out.					
60	Whenever I feel scared I act as strong person to other.					
61	I hide my insecurities by either shouting or storming out of the place or avoiding any communications.					
62	Whenever I am angry at my superior, I lash out at my subordinates or juniors.					

(*Contd.*)

Sl. No.	Question	Strongly Disagree -1	Disagree -2	Neutral -3	Agree -4	Strongly Agree -5
63	In my family, if I am angry at my elders I lock myself/ pick a fight with younger ones/ break something/ refuse meals.					
64	I divert my aggression or energy by playing rough sports like football or basketball.					
65	I cannot take criticism from anyone.					
66	I feel people are judgmental towards me, my behavior and my lifestyle.					
67	I feel anxious because people tend to judge me.					
68	I feel unlucky whenever I am unable to achieve a target or goal.					
69	I am immediately able to understand about right and wrong of myself.					
70	I am unable to accept my faults in presence of others.					
71	I am critical towards others task to improve them (even if they fail to appreciate my criticism).					
72	I keep up with my plans as per my opinion despite of other objecting it.					
73	I gain a deeper understanding of a problem before resolving it.					

(*Contd.*)

Sl. No.	Question	Strongly Disagree -1	Disagree -2	Neutral -3	Agree -4	Strongly Agree -5
74	I aim to resolve a problem as quick as possible.					
75	I analyze the shortcomings and failures in my behavior.					
76	I like to keep my insecurities to myself as I want to show my strong face only.					
77	I tell my family members 'they are nothing without me'.					
78	I tell my colleagues or friends 'they are nothing without me'.					
79	When I decide to go slow, in work or at home, I can easily procrastinate with deliberate calculation.					
80	I have fantastic memory of past.					
81	I suppress my urges to eat by adapting various diet plans.					
82	I try to control my desires such as shopping, eating at fancy places etc.					
83	I engross in binge watching online serials on Netflix, Hotstar etc.					
84	I engage in physically laborious tasks.					
85	I spend more than two hours in gym or other exercises forms.					

(*Contd.*)

Sl. No.	Question	Strongly Disagree -1	Disagree -2	Neutral -3	Agree -4	Strongly Agree -5
86	I engage in excessive actions such as party, exercise etc.					
87	I make wrong decisions at work place.					
88	I make wrong decisions in personal life.					
89	I take decision in my family whether I make the right or wrong decisions.					
90	I make trials and errors in life instead of listening to advices from others.					
91	I like to shift my tasks and responsibilities on others.					
92	I have a tendency to push my tasks beyond the timeline.					
93	I am a lazy person.					
94	I like to lay around instead of putting in laborious efforts.					
95	I keep repeating such tasks where I might lose money.					
96	I lose money and time on certain tasks such as share market, buying clothes or accessories etc.					
97	My friends and family members tell me that some of my behavior are inappropriate according to situation.					

(*Contd.*)

Sl. No.	Question	Strongly Disagree -1	Disagree -2	Neutral -3	Agree -4	Strongly Agree -5
98	I laugh on situations where people feel sad.					
99	I feel sad when others success is more than mine.					
100	I believe in investments whether it reaps me loss or gain does not matter to me.					
101	One should have contact with people who hold important positions.					
102	I choose to be friends and acquaintances with those who are famous, powerful and influential.					
103	To someone who is older than me, I do not hesitate in showing them their correct place with my supreme intelligence.					
104	I can argue, quarrel and make sure that I prove my perspective to people who are older or more experienced than myself.					
105	I like to compete with experienced people and pull them down.					
106	A true sign of intelligence is following the correct knowledge instead of making others follow it.					
107	If I don't prove my seniors/ teachers/elder ones wrong, I would lose my social credits.					

(Contd.)

Sl. No.	Question	Strongly Disagree -1	Disagree -2	Neutral -3	Agree -4	Strongly Agree -5
108	I get angry so fast on others and myself.					
109	I let my anger last for years.					
110	My anger subsides quickly.					
111	I take revenge from others for their wrong doings.					
112	I am told by others that I complicate things in my life.					
113	I think I am simple but my friends and family disagree.					
114	I have to earn a lot of money and make all my dreams come true.					
115	I want so much money that I face no problem in my future.					
116	I keep friendship with people who can bully or scare others.					
117	I have friends who can go through any limits for me.					
118	I start my job on time but get distracted and keep my job tasks pending.					
119	My phone and other gadgets and people distract me and waste my time.					
120	I feel inferior in company of my colleagues or peers.					

People with high pragnya quotient are likely to be less affected with triguna. They can prevent their indulgence in the three guna characteristics. So they have rational and experiential ability, and rational and experiential engagement.

Note

1. Gitanjali Roy, DCAH, Ph.D., Assistant Professor, Department of Psychology, Faculty of Education and Psychology, The Maharaja Sayajirao University of Baroda.

7
Mind is like a Mirror

Genius of Sigmund Freud

Mind is like a mirror; it gathers dust while it reflects. It needs the gentle breezes of Soul-Wisdom to brush away the dust of our illusions.[1] This was said by Helena Blavatsky more than 100 years ago. She was a spiritualist, in pursuit of ultimate reality. She indulged in occult practices that are irrelevant to contemporary times but her reflection is perennial. Sages happen to arrive at a realistic appraisal with a quantum jump.

On the other end, Sigmund Freud explored the mystery of the functioning of the mind. Until then, psychology as a separate discipline was unknown. Now, psychology as we have seen earlier has also matured to study the mind objectively. Several psychometric scores are now available.

Blavatsky spoke wisely in short and splendid words. Freud dissected and described in a discursive scientific mode. Both of them taken together are relevant. As a subtle and succinct metaphor and as verifiable with practice scientific mode. Therefore, the concepts taken as one are relevant to our discussion on contemporizing Pragnya.

This dissective divisive approach has been a departure from holism. Specialization has progressed so that not only psychology and philosophy are distinctly different disciplines but there are subdivisions of each of them. In the process an axiomatic truth is forgotten. In-depth understanding of any phenomenon in nature may need specialization in search.

However, the fact that the mind and body are separate entities is a certain illusion. Mind exists as long as a physically functioning brain in a physical body survives. So, we shall begin with the basic understanding that Mind-Body is a single entity.

Each individual is endowed with a certain number of brain cells. They communicate with each other and with various organs of the body through innumerable synapses and molecules of information substances. This material fact will determine the possibility of developing intellectual faculty. Genes would have dictated a predetermined inheritance. Yet, seed and soil are both important. A person brought up as uncouth and unsophisticated would be unsuitable to urbane company. If he has a brain capable of an IQ of more than 140, the person may not yield a psychometric assessment since he will be lacking in information. So, cultivation amounting to a cultural environment will also determine the outcome of personality.

A child gathers innumerable bits of information; based on that he develops concepts and faculty of enlarging them. By mature age, the baseline is established. Yet, there is a distinct feasibility to expand synaptic networks until senescence.

Life is full of vicissitudes. No man is an island. His own situation as well as the situation surrounding his societal structure does cause ups and downs. There the baseline of motivation is self-preservation. Generally the tendency observed in most individuals is to assert that he is infallible—not liable to make mistakes.

Ego is a psychic entity. So are id and superego. Id is an uncultivated, uncivilized archetypal factor that constantly urges the person to derive benefit regardless of social and mora restrictions. Super ego is functioning to control the irrationa demands of id. This causes a constant struggle in the mind. In the process, ego invents various kinds of psychic mechanisms—excuses. This is neurosis and it can certainly be wiped off by the person himself with recourse to his own Pragnya or may be by counseling and psychotherapy.

Defences of Ego

Ego provides dynamic drive to the functions of the individual. Drive can only be forceful when the power for the drive is applied surely and certainly. When ego is threatened with questions of uncertainty and likelihood of having made a mistake , drive is imperiled. Ego manipulates in such situations by taking recourse to several immature ways so as to reinforce the drive.

Let us examine some of the manipulations that ego assertion discovers to protect integral self image:

Immature Defenses of Ego

- **Projection:** An unsuccessful attempt culminating into a failure may be attributed to an external agency. A student who has not worked well enough is failed. His projection will attribute the failure to bad teaching. Even a personal factor such as feelings may also be attributed as an interference by those surrounding. This jars personal relationships by severe prejudice, rejection of intimacy, suspicion, hyper vigilance to external danger.
- **Blocking:** A person may present with an acceptable symptom socially and with the surroundings. This is commonly seen in Indian women. We have seen this happening numerous times when a woman would consult us with vague symptoms. It will require further prodding to bring them to the expression of their hidden motive to have a male child. The subject is subconsciously aware

but has successfully blocked the impulse from being aware about it.

- **Hypochondriasis:** A normal person takes recourse to complaining about physical symptoms for which there is no other explanation. A child may be reproached by the father. He may develop pain, migraine, loss of appetite, nausea, headache, weakness etc.
- **Passive Aggressive Behavior:** A person is feeble. He/she is surrounded by adverse situations but has no means of escape. Aggression towards an object expressed indirectly and ineffectively.
- **Regression:** It is axiomatic that a more powerful stimulus overcomes the feeble impulses. Empirical evidence may be derived by the fact that a child may have had a very happy childhood memory of studying in school. When faced with the enormity of pressure for providing a thesis for Ph.D. a person may experience depression. He himself may take to fantasizing about his happy childhood days. Regression in time may be used as a fantasy to experience previously experienced pleasant situations. This may also be applied as a progression in future to the possibilities of bright and happy situations to come.
- **Somatization:** Mind-Body is one. Intensity of neurotic symptoms may indeed progress to organic disorders. They are disorders of autoimmune process. Here the person has converted his psychological situations into such molecules of emotions. So, there is rejection of bodily self.
- **Acting out:** This is taking recourse to dramatics. The person may utilize metaphors. The dramatic act is to show off that he is not really affected by the situation.
- **Schizoid Fantasy:** Subject derives compensation in this mode for gratification and conflict resolution. Virtual imagination as a fantasy may be passed on as a reality. Subjects having this kind of experience are difficult to be

convinced that what they have imagined has really not occurred. Counseling turns out to be futile. Recourse may be taken to alternative psychotherapeutic measures such as hypnotherapy.

A real life story as an empirical evidence as follows:

A middle aged couple approached the therapist with the story. They said that they lived in isolation at the foot-end of a mountain. It was almost like living in a valley. Though they had no neighbors, some bad powerful men would descend from the mountains. While the husband was narrating the story, the wife went on consenting with yes at every sentence. 'Not only did they plunder our house, they raped my wife.' To this also the wife said yes.

They complained to the police and the police refused to believe them. This is conjugal schizoid fantasy.

- **Displacement:** In the interest of conflict resolution, attention is shifted from one pursuit to another alternative. A student changing the career option is a good empirical evidence.
- **Dissociation:** A temporary but drastic modification of character or sense of personal identity to avoid emotional distress. This is a borderline between neurosis and a psychiatric disorder.
- **Projective Identification:** The object of projection invokes in that person precisely the thoughts, feelings or behaviors projected. Empirical Evidence may be deduced by a lover identifying a photograph of some other article belonging to the beloved as real.
- **Megalomania:** Every human being of either sex has a location in family, society and other societal situations. Each of them may be empowering to a certain extent. A person suffering from megalomania comes to project to

oneself a larger than life image of his personality. Empirical evidence is best derived from modern history as:

- Jawaharlal Nehru in 1962 asked Indian Army to push off the Chinese. He had come to acquire a taller image of himself as the tallest statesman from Asia following the Bandung Conference. He led the non-aligned nations, China notwithstanding. There was a debacle which has come to be known as 'Himalayan Blunder'.
- Winston Churchill, after an alliance with the US forces, won the Second World War. He identified himself as The Winner. British people rejected him at the polls.

Redemption from severe depression could be made with efforts from his caring wife. She took him to the USA (This will emphasize the importance of displacement and dissociation as a therapy). Americans crowded paying high fees to hear Churchill and applauded him as a hero.

Mature Defenses

- **Controlling:** Most people have the need to be in charge of their own affairs. When confidence wanes, anxiety takes control. This results in excessive attempts to manage or regulate events or objects in the environment in the interest of minimizing anxiety and solving internal conflicts.
- **Anxiety:** Anxiety can be a motivation to pursue a goal in a steadfast way. When it aggravates, it impairs performance.
- **Altruism:** Constructive service to others that brings pleasure and personal satisfaction. There are numerous instances from history as well as of now. Smithsonian Institutes in Washington, Burroughs Wellcome Foundation and Bill and Melinda Gates Foundation illustrate the virtue of capitalism. Recent Covid pandemic

and the ravaging Tauke hurricane has brought about awakening of several kindred souls.

- **Anticipation and Rationalization:** Neurosis are amenable to cope with and to come over with self-help. Realistic planning for future discomfort. This can be done by anticipation. While one plans the future course of action, he is also aware about the mistakes that may have occurred. Instead of apportioning guilt to oneself or to others, rationalization with logical analysis yields self cure.
- **Humor:** Overt expression of ideas and feelings that gives pleasure to others. Ideas and feelings illustrated by a person of some mistakes that he has committed as silly mistakes that give humor to others.
- **Identification:** The unconscious modeling of one's self upon another person's character and behavior. Another idealistic model of one's imagination. This is frequently utilized by most young people to follow a model of their ideal, may be a movie star, a political leader or spiritual guru.

Above is a brief account of what Helena Blavatsky would have considered as a dust that is likely to be deposited over the shining mirror that is the mind. Numerous others such as compensation, transference, introjection, asceticism, sublimation, intellectualization, reaction formation and repression may be added to the above. We are risking a slight diversion from the main theme. This is because we have to emphasize how great a genius Freud had been. Asceticism and sublimation are well known in Indian tradition. However, Freud was a product of Western civilization. He derived inference from his patients. He had not travelled India, nor had he studied Indian traditions as Max Mueller in Germany did. Yet, Freud included asceticism and sublimation as mature defenses of ego.

Let us try to psychoanalyze how asceticism and sublimation could be mature defenses of ego.

Asceticism is the antithesis of ordinarily enjoyable needs and situations. Food is necessary for nourishing the body so that the mind may as well function well. Taste is an enjoyable pleasure. Greek Civilization invited peril when the Greeks heavily relied on this pleasure seeking enjoyment. When the stomach was full, they went to the toilet to vomit so that more food could be taken once again. It is elementary that this kind of attitude does not take a civilization forward. Leave alone making a person more satiated.

Asceticism aims at minimizing the bodily needs to be as frugal as possible. When the appetite is satiated, even starvation may be easy to endure. There are several shining empirical evidences to support this.

Mahatma Gandhi underwent fast for 21 days that stirred up the conscience of the entire nation. His last fast at the age of 75+ at Kolkata stopped the warring communities within a day when the law and order situation had failed altogether with authorities unable to control it. Vinoba Bhave at a ripe age realized that his body is not able to function, he gave up life voluntarily by fasting.

There is a well established tradition with Jain saints. Only at the beginning of this century, a Jain saint left his body after fasting for 140+ days. Wealthy community persons vied with each other to bid for the privilege to perform his last rites. That fetched a stupendous amount of money. That was for donation to the welfare at large.

Sublimation

How Sigmund Freud thought of this as mature defense defies our understanding. Freud is commonly known to lay people as an advocate of sex as the primary instinct, the driving motivation from infancy to old age. This is common and acceptable as a part of Western society. Bertrand Russell married for the fourth time after he had passed the age of 80. Will Durant married a teenager. She, Ariel Durant, was later to be included as a co-author to his voluminous work.

Nature wants to propagate the species. It happens *via* sexually driven behavior. Undoubtedly the drive is at times so powerful that it subjugates all other motives.

Yet, Indian and far Eastern traditions are ripe with everyday occurrences of sublimation of sex. Monks of several traditions including both sexes are worshipped as saints. This may be because they may have been very erudite but primarily because they have overcome a difficult drive and subjugated it. Best empirical evidence is the Dalai Lama.

Vatsayana, a Rishi, wrote *Kamasutra.* There the human sexual behaviour is narrated so as to guide a novice young youth. Now planning a family has emerged as a necessity for young youth. Why should they not be guided so as to better regulate their lives in accordance with their ambitions?

Blavatsky realized various aberrations of perceptions as dust on a spiritual quest. It is eulogized and practiced by theosophists numbering more than 15000 all over the world. On the other hand, the scientific genius of Freud arrived at this knowledge through validation with clinical practice; both ways are precious tools for the heritage of mankind since they provide an exit route from neurotic behavior. Once again, when this is done, Pragnya will restore its sunshine.

Eclipse of Pragnya

There are moments in the lives of most people when a sad situation arises, be it bereavement on account of the loss of a dear one, a failure in relationships, or a financial situation resulting in heavy loss. Environmental stresses also affect the mirror of the mind. Genetics may predispose certain people to depression. Psychiatrists keep busy in classifying depressions into categories.

At any given time, about 30 per cent of the population is known to have been suffering from depression. At such a time, energy is so depleted that the person sits on for a long, long time without any physical movement or even without thinking with a purpose. There is not enough energy even to open an envelope and read.

We call this depression an eclipse of Pragnya. There is a sure and certain way to get rid of this eclipse. Eclipse may pass off on its own as a change from a cold environment to summer days. It may also be helped with societal support from family and friends. Drugs do help, but they should only be taken under medical supervision. They can prompt the person to:

- Eat and drink optimally.
- Exercise twice a day.
- Stop using tobacco and certainly don't go to use addictive substances.
- Study and practice relaxation techniques.
- Examine your values and live by them.
- Reduce triggers of stress.

At this stage, we may say, the practice of certain mental exercises, such as progressive muscular relaxation, deep breathing exercise and mindfulness meditation are sure to help.

While meditation can be practiced with numerous techniques that will bring about profound implications, it may be reserved for those who want to shine their Pragnya better. For a depressed person in need of help, mindfulness meditation is elementary. A depressed person is over obsessed by the burden of numerous thought particles over his mind. When he minds his mind mindfully with mindfulness meditation, depression is sure to wane.

Mindfulness meditation is in vogue in the West as of now. Its origin is from Buddhist tradition. Training at source can be obtained from Tibetan monks at Dharamshala. But, several western investigators beginning with Herbert Benson have travelled long distances to understand relaxation response well.[2]

However, a natural tendency for the body to rejuvenate itself was even thought of by Claude Bernard as milieu interior. As an antithesis to the eclipse of Pragnya, Maharshi Patanjali has charted a path. Following this pathway, not only can one get rid of the eclipse fast, but also remain in perennial state of bliss.[3] When a meditator regularly practices as *sadhana*, his Pragnya remains as fresh as the flowers in spring. There are more and more pathways that are being decoded for rejuvenation of body and mind automatically.

Time honoured practice is to get away from stressful situations. Take leave. Go for holidays at naturally beautiful, open spaces at the mountains or sea or vast landscapes. Mother Nature unfolds several messages everyday. A widely used metaphor is that after a deep dark night, it is certain that the sunrise is going to be bright.

There are several measuring scales for depression, they also indicate a possibility of outcome. On the contrary, the scales for mental health are also available. They are on a positive side. The scales for various occupational stresses are numerous. A job may be precious. But when identified as a stressor, either a short gap or proceeding on leave may also suffice.

Personality profile of some depressed patients may reveal that they are obstinate. They firmly assert that others don't understand them well. Counseling such persons would take a long time and may involve additional psychotherapeutic measures.

Burnout that indicates exhaustion of energy leads to severe depression. However, a lamp that has exhausted its oil can always be relit by fresh supply and a car may also be refuelled to drive again.

A layperson may also understand the various levels of scales as provided by Holmes and Rahe as below.

1. Death of spouse (100)
2. Divorce (73)
3. Marital separation (65)
4. Jail term (63)
5. Death of close family member (63)
6. Personal injury or illness (53)
7. Marriage (50)
8. Fired at work (47)
9. Marital reconciliation (45)
10. Retirement (45)
11. Change in health of family member (44)
12. Pregnancy (40)
13. Sex difficulties (39)
14. Gain of new family member (39)
15. Business readjustment (39)
16. Change in financial state (38)
17. Death of close friend (37)
18. Change to a different line of work (36)
19. Change in number of arguments with spouse (35)
20. A large mortgage or loan (31)
21. Foreclosure of mortgage or loan (30)
22. Change in responsibilities at work (29)
23. Son or daughter leaving home (29)
24. Trouble with in-laws (29)
25. Outstanding personal achievement (28)
26. Spouse begins or stops work (26)
27. Begin or end school/college (26)
28. Change in living conditions (25)
29. Revision of personal habits (24)
30. Trouble with boss (23)
31. Change in work hours or conditions (20)
32. Change in residence (20)
33. Change in school/college (20)
34. Change in recreation (19)

35. Change in church activities (19)
36. Change in social activities (18)
37. A moderate loan or mortgage (17)
38. Change in sleeping habits (16)
39. Change in number of family get-togethers (15)
40. Change in eating habits (15)
41. Vacation (13)
42. Christmas (12)
43. Minor violations of the law (11).

Worst outcome for a depressed person is suicide. It happens when at the first flicker of energy, a depressed person gets hold of a lethal substance or weapon and is able to execute exit. This should be taken as a failure of civil society. Societal support is a natural due for all human beings at times of distress. As understanding of such situations will improve, suicide rate will diminish.

Even at the risk of repetition, the above account is a realistic picture of human situation that generally passes on as normal. The performance may be varied. It will be erroneous and at times harmful to run to a psychiatrist.

It is postulated that thoughts are floating particles in the bloodstream. Before a thought may be verbalized or expressed by behavior as body language, it is possible that an intricate chain of molecular biological exchanges would have taken place. We shall take a review of a few important molecules in the next chapter.

Notes

1. *Isis Unveiled*—Helena Blavatsky.
2. Herbert Benson, *The Relaxation Response*.
3. Patanjali *Yoga Sutra*, 1.48—Ritambhara tatra pragya.

8
Molecules of Emotion and Behaviour

Happy Molecules

Entire human genome was decoded by 2003. Surprisingly there are only about 30,000 genes that regulate metabolic processes. That includes protein metabolism too. A novel paradigm for scientific advancement and understanding has emerged known as Bioinformatics.[1]

Proteins are the building blocks of all organs. They are also involved in transferring information as well as in storage of memory and its recall. For understanding what molecules may constitute a structural mechanism for Pragnya seems to be an impossible task. It is not necessary as well. A description of a few molecules that are responsible for different kinds of emotions and mood would suffice.

Unconscious mind is a demiurgic dynamic force. It drives the emotions. Emotions propel action. So let us understand the various molecules that are influencing the primitive brain that is thalamus, hypothalamus, limbic system, and pituitary gland.[2]

Endorphin

Endorphin produces 'euphoria' similar to the effect of exogenous morphine; since it is endogenous to body, therefore, the name, endorphin. Endorphin was the first of these substances. While it is secreted by physical pain, it is responsible for causing a sense of pleasure and joy in various situations including love and sex. Masochistic, narcissistic and sadistic traits have their roots with the association of pleasurable experiences that would have been derived through endorphin levels earlier. Endorphin secretion gets triggered and, an unfortunate connection in the brain is established in the Pavlovian model. Catharsis and crying helps since it stimulates endorphin secretion. Painful relationships get tolerated or even sustained because the brain has learned to expect good feelings.

Following case history illustrates the role of endorphin release related memory encoding leading to a stereotype behavior.

A newly married couple came for therapy. The woman was depressed after marriage though marriage was with her explicit consent. She would burst out into sobs after love making. The husband and his family were caring and, concerned. Yet, the depression would not abate.

Psychodynamic exploration revealed a premarital relationship which the woman had taken seriously: her paramour was just flirting. They had slept together and the woman had experienced ecstasy at the climax. When the boy plainly told about his casual attitude and moved away to Australia, she accepted the situation and, got married.

However, the boy continued to flirt. He would call her from Australia and make love talk. She would derail. We called up the boy and suggested to the boy that if he really loved the girl, he must not call her now.

This change, along with a strategy for selective ablation of past, substitution of euphoria with pain and time progression to happy family building almost restored her; till the boy returned to the city to get married and invited her to the marriage. In spite of desistance and warning from the therapist, she attended the marriage and, crashed once again.

Wise learn from the mistakes of others, fools from their own; but idiots who have experienced euphoria of a bygone endorphin release situation would not learn ever. Then a psychodrama of confrontational therapy was enacted and, it worked. So, of course, with help even idiots do learn to re-modulate their endorphins.

Dopamine

Dopamine is a neurohormone. It is responsible for the awake state. It plays a major role in the motivational component of reward-motivated behavior. It is also released by the hypothalamus. It has many functions in behavior and cognition such as voluntary movements, motivation, punishment and reward and prolactin production inhibition. It is rated to play a role in pain processing in multiple levels of the central nervous system. Dopamine increases general arousal and goal directed behavior and, decreases latent inhibition; all three effects increase the creative drive of idea generation.

Melatonin

Melatonin is secreted into the blood by the pineal gland in the brain. It is best secreted during the early hours of sunrise; before dawn. Therefore, melatonin secretion is least affected by emotions or external stimuli except the phases of the sun.

Melatonin is a geroprotector. Melatonin receptors appear to be important in mechanisms of learning and memory such as long-term potentiation (LTP). In perimenopausal women it produces an improvement in thyroid function and gonadotropin levels, restores fertility and menstruation and prevents the depression associated with menopause. Melatonin is an effective preventive treatment for migraine in some cases and, since it ameliorates circadian misalignment, it is the only drug for jet lag after travel. It is an anti-oxidant and suppressant of tumour development. Melatonin acts as a mild hypnotic. It is also applied in treating depression and seasonal affective disorder.

A team led by Bhaskar Vyas and Renu Sharma, comprising of various disciplines have engaged at M.S. University in fundamental research (2013-14) in the role of melatonin in hypnosis. There are 2 genes that regulate the production of the hormone by pineal gland. It is postulated that these genes get up-regulated during hypnosis. It will be ideal to study the activation of melatonin genes before and after hypnosis. However, the research on gene expression is highly expensive. Therefore, with limited funding from the surplus of 9th National Conference of Indian Society of Clinical and Experimental Hypnosis at Vadodara, the current research is likely to provide path breaking findings for melatonin metabolism. Though a single session of hypnosis did not show any significant increase in melatonin level, it was found to have a significant increase in subject's practicing some kind of meditation.[3]

Oxytocin

Oxytocin causes the feeling of being safe and bonded in social situations. It acts as a neuro-modulator in the brain. In lactating mothers it causes flow of milk. It is important for cervical dilation before birth and causes contractions during the second and third stages of labor. There is correlation of oxytocin with human bonding; increase in trust, and decrease in fear are attributed to the hormone. Certain learning and memory functions are impaired by centrally administered oxytocin. Oxytocin is involved in the initiation of maternal behaviour. Oxytocin inhibits the development of tolerance to various addictive drugs (opiates, cocaine, alcohol) and reduces withdrawal symptoms.

Serotonin

Serotonin produces the feeling of being respected and is responsible for feeling proud. Sense of etiquette is derived from serotonin. GI tract is responsible for 90 per cent of serotonin secretion. It has receptors all over the body.

Amygdale nucleus in hypothalamus monitors appropriateness to the extent of what and how to dress at what occasion. It can be said that the external appearance of a person that may exude a personality profile is determined by serotonin.

Above molecules are the real determinants of our happy personality profile at a given moment. Presence of appropriate proportions for most of the time will generate a happy person. That is the reason why the molecules are commonly called 'Molecules of Happiness—Happy Molecules'.

Prolific exuberance of above molecules produces a charming personality that spreads charm all around. The very presence of a person in a group makes a difference. True happiness radiates happiness all around. That is, indeed, charisma.

We shall discuss how to maintain proper balance of happy molecules in the body later. Life is bound to have some bad times. In this situation, the primary animal instinct is either to fight or to flee from the situation. Determinant principal hormone for this response is cortisol.

Cortisol

Cortisol is the stress hormone. It triggers different survival behaviors depending on whether it is paired with low blood sugar, or the presence of an unpleasant situation, or social exclusion. The actions of cortisol are best summarized as fight or flight response. Meditation converts the response to flow.

The effects on mood, behaviour and emotion during a period of high stress vary from individual to individual. The personality of the individual decides his response to stress, whether the person responds with a fighting attitude, prefers to flee from the fight or decides to flow with the times.

However, all of these responses do require a focused attention. An individual undergoing high levels of stress experiences peak attention. There may be associated euphoria as well.

Our present day lifestyle has inherited stress from 20th century. Hans Selye, as a medical student decoded what he called as general adaptation syndrome. A single minded pursuit of the research made Selye to forget filing income tax returns. It produced so much stress that he died due to stress in 1976!

His classic survives as a small book—Stress of Life. The importance of this short book may be gauged by the fact that as of today references regarding research on stress can only be catalogued into a 1000 page volume.

Note

Cortisol is released with a diurnal cycle and its release is increased in response to stress and low blood-glucose concentration. It functions to increase blood sugar through gluconeogenesis, to suppress the immune system, and to aid in the metabolism of fat, protein, and carbohydrates.

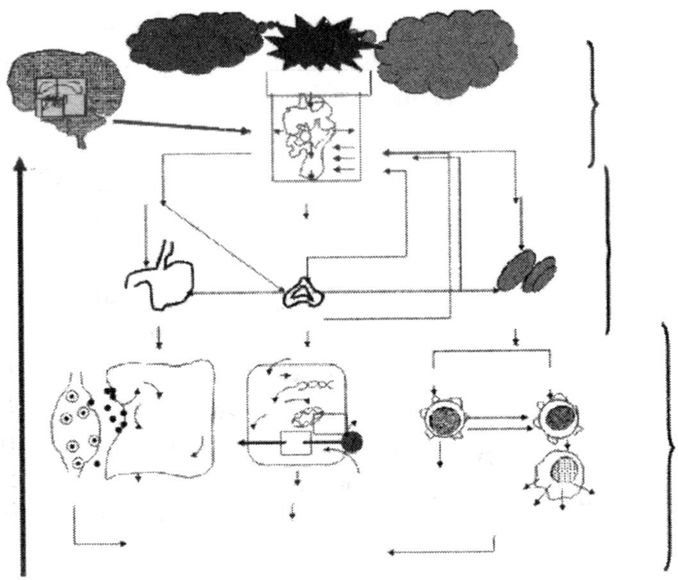

Fig. 7.1: Psychosomatic Medicine Theory—E. Rossi.

Stressors are perceived by the mind. They can be external such as extreme cold or extreme heat. Modern lifestyle is geared to produce stress. Ordinarily an inflammatory process only may begin to produce stress hormones; persistently perceived stress may also generate high levels of cortisol.

Cortisol is thus an anti-inflammatory agent but also reduces immunity.

Survival builds without effort or intent because neurochemicals pave pathways. The ability of a program for meditation lies in elucidating a particular phenomenon as a strategic tool in eliciting a desired response.

It follows, therefore, that Pragnya undulations can be minimised or even eliminated by meditation. Numerous strategies for meditation have evolved and are in the process for refinement with neuroscientific basis. Once upon a time this was an exclusive prerogative of Rishis living in forests and having followers that resided at ashrams over 12 years. A revolutionary change was initiated by Maheshyogi—TM guru, himself a scientist by education. He was the first to dispense a meditative program as per a short course of four to eight sessions. There was a fee, mostly affordable by all.

We believe that meditation by whatever name—to use the phrases by Patanjali, namely *Savikalpa* or *Nirvikalpa*—will enhance Pragnya scores.

Currently, various *Ashramas* and meditation centers are propagating Patanjali. Good people do not lie; as whatever and wherever the rain falls, it leads to the sea.

Notes

1. Rossi, E., Rossi, K., A. *Chapter in Creative Consciousness, A New Bioinformatics Paradigm for the Theory*, Research, and Practice of Therapeutic Hypnosis.
2. Vyas, B., Vyas, R., *et al. Indian Handbook of Hypnotherapy*, 4th Edition, pp. 36-38.
3. Dave, A., *et al.*, "Physiological Estimation of Melatonin Levels in Normal Indian Adults", *Post Hypnosis and Yoga Practitioners.*
4. Hans Selye, *Stress of Life*, 1956.

9

Brain Function is (W)holistic

It Functions as a Whole

We revert back, once again, to Rishi Charak. We have begun our endeavor to better understand what he conceptualized shortly as a composite admixture of *Dhi*—intellect, *Dhruti*—Patience and *Smruti*—memory. We have further expanded the concept to attitude as a personality profile derived from *Gunas—Satva, Rajas* and *Tamas.* While patience as a component of Pragnya is better discussed elsewhere and so is attitude, in this chapter we are exploring the neurological foundations of intellect as well as expansion of intellectuation and memory.

Roger Sperry, a neurosurgeon, was intensely focused as to how to help epilepsy patients. Now, epilepsy has two variants; Petitmal and grand mal. Both involve convulsions for a short time. Former involves only a part of the body. Generally, it is not dangerous. Grand mal begins with an aura—premonition. The person has only a few minutes to find a safe place to lie down. Premonitions do not arrive at a definite time or place. It may happen that a person walking on the footpath is noticed to have suddenly fallen down and he is convulsing. Or a woman who is cooking happens to fall on a fireplace. For a while the persons remain unconscious, in spite of severe injury or severe burn. At that time, there were no effective drugs or alternate therapeutic measures to treat epilepsy.

Roger Sperry was focused on finding a surgical intervention. As a neurosurgeon he would have liked to excise or extirpate the focus at which epilepsy begins. It was known that by some unknown stimulus an area in the motor cortex of one of the hemispheres gets activated. Progression rapidly happens so as the entire motor cortex of the affected hemisphere is involved. That side of the body happens to have seizures that rapidly progresses to the other side of the motor cortex. Consequently, the whole body is gripped with epilepsy. Even after stoppage of convulsions, the person remains unconscious for a long time.

Even if it was possible to localize the motor area that initiated firing the stimulus, its excision would mean loss of motor function to the part that was innervated and controlled by this area. But Sperry found that initiation began on one side of the body and later it went to the other side. That provided a sound clue that two hemispheres must have been in communication. Obvious, visible link is corpus callosum.

Let us revise elementary understanding about what constitutes our brain. Brain has two hemispheres, right and left. Each of them has control over motor and sensory stimuli on the alternate side of the body. This was long established before Sperry conducted initial experiments.

Corpus callosum is the connecting link between two hemispheres. The **corpus callosum** is a wide and thick bundle of nerve fibres and without any nerve cells. Since, it does not contain any nerve cell, it is obvious that the axonal fibres would be transferring information to and fro to both the hemispheres. Since there is no localization of any other particular function to corpus callosum, Sperry thought that its severance would only entail a break in the communication between the hemispheres. There will be no loss of function.

Sperry conducted initial experiments with monkeys. This was needed so that such a surgery would be safe and would not leave any permanent side effects. The premise came true. Monkeys not only survived sophisticated surgery but apparently did not have any derangement of functions of the brain.

In his experiments on monkeys Sperry found that, if the corpus callosum were severed, the connectivity between two hemispheres was lost. But each cerebral hemisphere would retain its ability to learn, but that what had been learned by one hemisphere was not available to the other.

Having established the safety in monkeys, Sperry dared to act to help epilepsy patients. Here again it was found that commissurotomy was a safe surgery, without any apparent side effects. Again on a closer loop, the patients were found to have been normal. But Sperry observed, in his own words, on the hemispheres of the brain, that it is "indeed a conscious system in its own right, perceiving, thinking, remembering, reasoning, willing, and emoting, all at a characteristically human level, and both the left and the right hemisphere may be conscious simultaneously in different, even in mutually conflicting, mental experiences that run along in parallel".

Sperry was the first ever to perform commissurotomy on humans. He was awarded the Nobel Prize for Physiology and Medicine. Thereafter, commissurotomy had been carried out in a number of patients suffering from severe, intractable epilepsy. The patients showed an improvement as well as a decrease in the frequency of epileptic seizures with statistical significance. No one could demonstrate with psychological test methods any impairment at all in the patients' ability to perceive and learn.

Sperry followed up the progress of his patients for a long time. He observed that *each cerebral hemisphere in his patients had its own world of consciousness and was entirely independent of the other with regard to learning and retention. Moreover, each*

had its own world of perceptual experience, emotions, thoughts and memory out of reach of the other cerebral hemisphere.

Nobel Prize citation for Roger Sperry has this narration:

> The *isolated left hemisphere* is concerned with abstract thinking, symbolic relationships and logical analysis of details, particularly relationships between objects. It can speak, write and make mathematical calculations; in its general function it is analytical and it is like a computer. It is also the more aggressive, executive, leading hemisphere. The *right hemisphere* is mute and generally lacks the possibility to communicate with the outside world. It is, as Sperry expresses it, "a passive, silent passenger who leaves the driving of behaviour mainly to the left hemisphere". Because of its muteness, the right hemisphere has so far been completely inaccessible for experimental studies, and also, as a consequence of this, has been considered as being entirely subordinate to the left hemisphere. Through Sperry's investigations, he revealed that the right hemisphere, contrary to what one previously thought, is clearly superior to the left hemisphere in many respects. It has the capacity for constructive thinking, spatial and temporal consciousness and comprehension of abstract relationships. It is also the superior hemisphere when it comes to interpreting auditory impressions and in comprehension of music; it can better recognize melodies and better distinguish voices and intonations. In other respects, however, the right hemisphere is lacking in respect to the left. It lacks almost entirely the ability to calculate and can only perform simple additions up to 20. It completely lacks the power to subtract, multiply or divide.

It can read and comprehend the meaning of simple, monosyllabic nouns but cannot perceive the import of adjectives or verbs. It cannot write. It is entirely superior to the left hemisphere when it comes to space perception and reproducing three-dimensional pictures.

The 21st century will be remembered as the century of the left brain dominated people. Computers and computations have given a thrust not only to the speed of working but also thinking. Artificial intelligence has already arrived on the horizon. Robots have started doing menial tasks so that human beings may engage in more intelligent work. However, when Sperry finished his research, he had observed that the structure, locus and initiation of consciousness in the brain are yet not established.

Sperry himself was aware about the limits of his research since it did not cover consciousness. There were scientific limitations of that time, namely, (a) electroencephalography studies were not done on commissurotomy patients. (b) functional magnetic resonance images—fMRI were not available at that time. These shortcomings are being taken care of now. Further research has shown that during meditative states, brain function studied with electroencephalography converts to generate alpha waves. Here also a question remained unanswered scientifically: if it were possible to induce alpha waves artificially, would that be a meditative state?

What Sperry found as a silent area in the prefrontal cortex was silent as per Sperry's interpretation since it did not generate a motor response. fMRI studies have shown that during and after meditative states the prefrontal cortex starts 'waking up'. There is increased brain blood flow that indicates functionality. Considering Sperry's inference as established science, it can be inferred that the prefrontal cortex was doing some abstract work that cannot be shown by movement of any part of the body. This gives us a simple derivation that the prefrontal cortex is involved in abstract thinking. We shall now see how this hardcore scientific data may be applied to a soft science—psychology.

Roger Sperry was focused on anatomical structures so as to surgically alter their role. We have seen that Sigmund Freud has conceptualized psychological, hypothetical structures, viz. ego, super ego, and id. Freud and his followers postulated that it is the **unconscious mind** that is the primary source of **human behavior**. Like an iceberg, the most important part of the **mind** is the part you cannot see.

Sperry was focused on cerebral hemispheres. Yet, he omitted the prefrontal cortex. At that time, it seemed to have no significance. Now it is established that the prefrontal cortex has special functions.

We now know that prefrontal cortex has functional abilities such as:

> There is an integral link between a person's will to live and his personality. It has been implicated in executive functions, such as planning, short term memory and decision making. Intense brain-storming may be involved in decision-making. A person would need a wide range of screening with moral, ethical and social considerations. It will also involve foresight about the outcome.
>
> Financial implications should also be involved. Complex situations may arise in relationships that may affect the entire lifestyle of the person. It differentiates among conflicting thoughts and various options, it projects to the futuristic possibilities, working toward a defined goal, it evaluates the consequences of an expected outcome and social control. The frontal cortex supports creativity.

> Every person has a right to live happily. Happiness depends on right and wrong, good and bad choices and also on creating better alternatives so that the choice may become better and the best has to be decided by several algorithms. This kind of thinking process obviously will involve intense and complex abstract thinking. Let us label that process as wisdom. Wisdom lies in masterful administration of even unforeseen.

Functions of the prefrontal cortex also involve personality expression, moderating social behavior and controlling certain aspects of speech and language. It is supposed to be harbouring spiritual personality traits associated with compassion, philanthropy and abstract guidance in esoteric matters. It is thought to be controlling the orchestration of thoughts and actions. This is in consonance to be a wise person.

It will be no exaggeration to assume that most creative inventive thoughts first arise in the prefrontal cortex. To put it succinctly; the prefrontal cortex is the wise man within. We have only made a recent acquaintance scientifically with the prefrontal cortex but it was there all along. There is a segment of thalamus that projects its way into the prefrontal cortex. The thalamus portion, named as mediodorsal nucleus of the thalamus, is associated with memory. From an evolutionary point of view, the thalamus as a whole is considered as the primitive brain. It links hypothalamus, again a part of the primitive brain, and pituitary gland, the maestro of endocrine orchestra. Thus, the wisdom of the prefrontal cortex can be well assumed to have a very wide and far acumen as seen from neurological aspects as well.

The anatomical structure of the prefrontal cortex indicates that there is a rich density of neuronal population, without localization in any particular area. So, the entire prefrontal cortex may be considered as the seat of Pragnya.

Even if it was thought that about 2 per cent of the human population is creatively engaged, it may amount to exaggeration. However, given an opportunity most human beings can work towards working with their whole brain. Physicists would provide good empirical evidence when they view their inventions not only mathematically but also with aesthetics. To quote a few:

- Paul Dirac was a theoretical physicist. He has the distinction of being the youngest person to be awarded the Nobel Prize, and he has further distinguished himself by being awarded the Nobel Prize 3 times! He was asked how he would verify the veracity of his hypothesis. He replied,
  I work mainly with paper and pencil. Mathematics is precisely deductive logic. It works with numericals and equations that cannot be altered at all. But, inference may be deduced further if a hypothesis is proposed mathematically.
  When I experienced that there is an easy, almost poetic flow to my equations, it is most likely true. Truth is beautiful.
- Subhramanyan Chandrashekhar was awarded the 1983 Nobel Prize for Physics. The wide range of his research in physics included astronomy, gravitational fields collision, and even hydrodynamics etc.!
- Yet, he wrote a classic in philosophy, namely, "Truth and Beauty. Aesthetics and motivations in science". The conclusion arrived at by him in this book is that truth and beauty are synonymous.[1]
- A letter from Albert Einstein to a fellow physicist, Hadamard amply describes the process of creativity. From **The Mathematician's Mind: The Psychology of Invention in the Mathematical Field**—

"(A) The words or the language, as they are written or spoken, do not seem to play any role in my mechanism of thought. The psychical entities which seem to serve as elements in thought are certain signs and more or less clear images which can be "voluntarily" reproduced and combined. There is, of course, a certain connection between those elements and relevant logical concepts. It is also clear that the desire to arrive finally at logically connected concepts is the emotional basis of this rather vague play with the above-mentioned elements. But taken from a psychological viewpoint, this combinatory play seems to be the essential feature in productive thought—before there is any connection with logical construction in words or other kinds of signs which can be communicated to others.

(B) The above-mentioned elements are, in my case, of visual and some of muscular type. Conventional words or other signs have to be sought for laboriously only in a secondary stage, when the mentioned associative play is sufficiently established and can be reproduced at will.

(C) According to what has been said, the play with the mentioned elements is aimed to be analogous to certain logical connections one is searching for.

(D) Visual and Motor. In a stage when words intervene at all, they are, in my case, purely auditive, but they interfere only in a secondary stage, as already mentioned.

(E) It seems to me that what you call full consciousness is a limit case which can never be fully accomplished. This seems to me connected with the fact called the narrowness of consciousness (Enge des Bewusstseins)."

- Beethoven has become an immortal symbol of creating music. He composed the first two of his symphonies when he was getting more and more hard of hearing. Next four symphonies were composed when he was completely deaf. Had he been born a deaf child, he would have also been a mute child. He would not have been able to read or write his mother tongue, leave aside composing music. Since he had learnt music and gone ahead with composing two symphonies, even with partial hearing, it is obvious that he could have done so by recalling stored memories of music that he may have heard during his lifetime.

  There are two auditory nerves on each side of the brain that end in an auditory centre. The centre relays the information to the centre for hearing in the temporal region of each hemisphere. This only provides a pathway to pass the sound to each hemisphere. But, whether it is noise, useful communication, gibberish or sweet music is to be ascertained by a recall of previous experience. Beethoven would have composed his music with that kind of internal recall from each side of the brain as well as what note would create better music would have been an input by prefrontal cortex.

  The symphony created by Beethoven was the kind that never before had been created. What has never occurred before is an abstract concept. That kind of abstraction is not a recall but an inventive creation. The neurological process would have involved communication with innumerable synapses, finally, to arrive at a particular musical note.

  Later in his life, after he became a celebrity, Pablo Picasso painted ten abstract paintings. They sold out at a fabulous price. Then Picasso was to declare, he was fooling people, there is nothing much in the paintings.

The lovers of the art were left aghast. But, critics came to rescue. They pronounced that the paintings were indeed the work of a genius. Only the genius Picasso seemed to have gone awry. May be old age was eclipsing Pragnya of Picasso!

- This real life story is about Pt. Jasraj who passed away in 2020.
- At an adolescent age, he was content to be an accomplished Tabla player to his vocalist elder brother. Tabla is a percussion instrument that measures time with mathematical, numerical beats. Tabla at that time was considered not much of an art.

  At one concert, Jasraj happened to sit down next to the vocalist. The organizer chided him with an insult; your place is to sit on a lower seat, you cannot equate yourself to the vocalist musician. The insult went deep into his heart. He was so hurt that he learnt a lesson from this suffering. He decided to be a vocalist!

  Classical Indian music is sung as spontaneously created. This is true as far as initial rendering is concerned. There is so much liberty to the artist that he is identified by the style that he generates. Further rendering does require playing to the rhythm as decided between the percussionist and the vocalist.

  After more than 70 years of career, he has achieved almost an immortality in Indian classical music. Not only did he perform all over India, but also in the Western world. Later in life, his musical style turned spiritual as well. He began recital by first dedicating his rendering so as to provide peace and prosperity by invocation to Bhagwan Vishnu. However, Jasraj's spirituality was not confined to Hindu gods. He has also sung in praise of Allah!

  Would this empirical evidence not suffice as a proof that spirituality is also a (w)holistic function?

Research by Sperry was aimed at providing a solution to epilepsy. Commissurotomy has been subsequently performed on innumerable patients. They benefited. Now, better and better drugs are available so that such sophisticated surgery may not be needed! It is likely that psychotherapy using hypnosis may also obviate seizures.

In contrast, most of us have our corpus callosum intact. This thick bundle of white matter transmits several million gigabytes of information at every second between two hemispheres. It is upto various centres that they impinge upon to further process and reverberate into a fresh output. Thus Sperry's research has also generated an antithesis that normal people would live normally and may also arrive at wise decisions by communication between two hemispheres.

Roger Sperry was awarded the Nobel Prize for his observations on hemispheres. As a by-product of this research, it provided a first ever opportunity to study the functionality of each hemisphere separately. Based on his results, numerous publications describing separately distinct function of each hemisphere appeared. Several publications in book form or online on the internet, such as 'One Head, Two Brains' did sell highly. They provided wonder and awe but were misleading.

Profile of personality distinctly different and at times opposites to each other, are summarized in a table below:

Table 9.1

Type A—LEFT	Type B—RIGHT
Always moving	Not concerned about time
Walks rapidly	
Eats and talks rapidly	
Impatient	Patient
Does more than one thing at a time	No bragging
Cannot cope with leisure	plays for fun, not to win

(Contd.)

Type A—LEFT	Type B—RIGHT
Obsessed with numbers	Relaxes without guilt
Measures success by quantity	Has no pressing deadlines
Aggressive	Mild mannered
Competitive	Not in a hurry
Constantly under time pressure	

Split brain theory has fascinated psychologists globally. So much so that a personality classification of type A for the left brain dominance and personality type B for right brain dominance is still currently in vogue.

Laymen including psychologists of yesteryears said that a person may have a personality profile as extrovert or introvert. Basically, this is still true for laymen to judge. However, Roger Sperry's interpretations were on patients—surgically operated. So the research conclusions are lopsided that cannot be applied to the normal individuals that constitute a huge mass of humanity.

The present day societal structures are based on a value system that assigns high price to the Type A personality profile. This personality profile is associated with logical, rational behaviour that uses a step-by-step, sequential approach to thinking, learning, problem solving, and decision making.

Most brilliant people opt for technology and science based careers. However, price and value are two different properties. A software, however ingeniously it may have been designed, will have a short lifespan of only a few years. Paintings of various shades belonging to a wide range of schools adorn museums across the world. They are viewed time and again so as to send the viewer into ecstasy! Full of amazement! And derive different meanings and inspirations at different times!

Creative Process

Before discussing creative process further, therefore, let us elucidate how Pragnya and Pragnya quotient would correlate with creative process.

We take recourse once again to Charak's axiomatic statement. He has said that Pragnya has 3 components: Intelligence, Patience to hold on and Memory that would entail even deeply embedded into various layers of the mind that may encompass even unconscious mind. Each of these three can be further dissected into different segments that will finally provide a composite holistic understanding as to what will constitute Pragnya.

- Obviously only a person with high intelligence quotient can engage into a creative process. However, the direction of a new creation will be decided by what direction a new innovation or final product would take. May it be a new tool for a carpenter or a new app for a software scientist or a painting when finished or how a musical note for a music composer would sound melodious. Thus, intentionality is an essential initiator to the creative process.
- Depending upon the education and the training to execute an idea, an intelligent person can only mull over in the mind as to how to rotate or change the sequence of various phrases since change of syntax can altogether change the meaning of the entire composition. It will be even more difficult to grasp the semantics of a new creation.
- Let us illustrate with painting of Mona Lisa. A novice in art appreciation will pass by the painting as that of a beautiful woman. When he has pondered over the painting, he may see that the painting is a masterpiece since the smile of Mona Lisa is truly mystical. Does it radiate inner joy, truly tranquil peace, or she is simply happy? While a few would want to muse as to the deeper content still it suddenly may dawn upon the viewer that not only is the painting of a beautiful woman with a mystical smile, but she signifies the entire process of creation with the background as depicted faintly.

Semantics

First, we shall endeavor to explicate the notion of creative visualization as a semantic feature of thinking. Human consciousness is creative. Creativity needs semantic characterization (but the meaning may be implicit or hidden and may not be discernable at all) in order to show that it is intrinsic to human thought. A creative visual state is visualized in our imagination. Visualization is a mode of experiencing thoughts. We shall review both semantics and syntax as a creative process.

Creative visualization is one of the modes of 'visual experience'. A person experiences imageries in his/her imagination. Imagination itself is a process of transforming thoughts. Imagination as it has been usually understood is a power to call up images. When this realization grows into something new, may be a novel idea, a new concept, a better way of doing things, or into an aesthetically pleasing product, the visualization may be termed creative.

Creativity is initially formed in imagination. A creative genius—or an ordinary individual experiencing hypnosis—is very much conscious about sensing creative ideas that form in his imagination. In his imagination he tries to conceive imageries for a better representation. At the beginning, he *feels* about it but his intention is to have a *perspicuous* representation that is more significant.

Taking the illustration to a painting. How would a painter understand or judge that now the painting is complete? Adding even a dot would change the entire idea that the painter may have imagined in his unconscious mind. Therefore, herein lies the process of creativity. What was visualized in imagination has to be produced exactly through the creative process. This transition from imagination to the obvious will determine that it has not only undergone intelligent understanding but during the creative process the creator has subjected the creation to his own inner semantic appreciation. Representation involves, memory, recall, emotion, feelings, sentiments, revalidation, recapitulation through which the artist in any subject nurtures the gestate images.

A creative state undergoes *transformation* in the process of formulating new ideas. The content of a creative state gets modified till the artist realizes that the piece of art is complete. The modification is a sustained interplay among the emerging imageries and their applications. The process will be handled by both visual centers in the orbital cortex; subsequently, an entire brain scan will be needed for recall and revalidation. The prefrontal cortex will be involved to discriminate whether it is good, bad or worthless. Integrate logical processing through induction and deduction will be applied. Thus when an execution is determined, the entire brain would have scanned conscious, subconscious and unconscious processes in the mind. For instance, we can think of a musician trying to put notes in the instrument. The person repeats the notes again and again till he gets fine-tuned playing the notes. The painter works on the canvas repeatedly with colours and lines many times till he is satisfied. The process of modification, therefore, is a shift from an *imperfect* creative state to a *perfect* one. The modification of mental states *persists in time* which could be linguistically translated in terms of the verb 'to happen' or 'may happen'.

When a person is involved in creating something new, he is aware of the experience that he undergoes. The feeling of that sensibility is a mode of realizing something and then expressing it. The form of sensing and form of describing is nothing but a process of transformation of experience, which results in joy, pride, something new which we call transforming too. This transformation of thoughts is a part of thinking whether it is verbal to visual or visual to verbal. The content of visual experience of thought and the expression of the experience of thoughts are meaningfully connected.

There are perceptual experiences, they have intentionality, their intentional content is propositional in form; they have the direction from the mind to the world direction. This can happen in both the directions. The properties which are specified by their intentional content are not in general literally properties of perceptual experiences. The properties may take altogether a different form. Since the process is bidirectional, verification continues and a modification may also be simultaneously done. Visualization may occur through symbols. Images are just a two-dimensional picture. Any symbol of whatever kind would be portent with meaning as per the sensibilities of the creator.

There is an intentional feature embedded in structuring the content of experience. He maintains that the semantic characterization of the content of experience flows from the *intentionality* of consciousness. A creative person keeps on his creative process at a subconscious level or he may engage in a reverie so as to generate a different state of consciousness—Trance. When creation is complete, Eureka!—Aha! experience is the proof that creation has vitality and validity.

An artiste's willingness to have a perspicuous representation of thought signifies not only the pictorial features of thoughts but also the process of experiencing. The content of the experience is to give a *meaning* to the piece of art.

For instance, while playing a few notes, a musician keeps on modifying the notes for a better tune. Here, being conscious of tuning and opting for possible modifications are due to the self-referential feature of consciousness. That is, intentionality is involved in showing the directedness from *mind to the world*, i.e. playing of the notes shows flow of intentionality from thought to action; whereas, listening to the tuning shows the *world to the mind* direction. The intention flows from the *subject pole* to the *object pole* and *vice versa* which constitutes the field of experience. The shift of visual fields would show the manifoldness of intentionality transforming the visual fields and entering into different realms of experience. That is precisely how one talks about the experience of *solitude* in the presence of others. Although the shifting of visual field is the process of the change in sequence of thoughts, it is still due to the intentionality that acts in the *background* of consciousness.

Syntax

Every researcher/creative person rests on the shoulders of numerous people. A scientific invention comes into existence resting on proven theorems and verified experiments. Painters are now 'trained' at several fine arts faculties so are the musicians taught at the universities. Thus, learning is a syntactical process. No man is an island. Connecting to an idea that has already been verified may also generate a new invention.

Cognitive science discards the traditional notion of thinking as a conscious activity. Rather thinking is a mental process which can be explained with relation to brain processes. The representational features of thoughts are representations of physical events in the brain. That experience is caused by the neurophysiology of the brain. The ability to create images is quite subjective, or what is thought by a creative person is quite different from other creative persons. The comprehension of images is very important to produce a veritable hypothesis. If a stimulus fails to stimulate, then it fails to generate responses. The above discussion suffices to prove that mental images are a logical construction of certain elements of brain processes. The reality of mental images or the formatting capacity of mental representation is rooted in the neurophysiological structures and functions of the brain.

Mental states are inferential states. Mental states embody certain properties for transforming the stimuli into images once they are simulated. Extensional characterization in terms of physics or physiology should be amenable to explanation and prediction. Functioning of the innumerable neurons in the brain at a particular point is so chaotic (in the sense the new branch of physics of chaos) that it seems almost impossible today to decipher as to how content, meaning and intentionality come out of that function.

Although actual occurrence of quantum phenomena in neural networks is still lacking proof, should the developments of measuring devices in experimental physics were to confirm them, randomness and chance occurrences that characterize the quantum events would qualify the creative images to be the end product of such randomness. The concern lies in the incompleteness of the physicalist' agenda in their extensional explanation as well as the exclusion of the first person perspective to understanding experience. We shall be then forced to another aspect of cognition; what is joy and beauty is a work of a creative mind; what is ugly and dangerous is the product of schizophrenia.

This exemplifies propositional attitude psychology. PAP explicates the semantic properties of mental states pictured with the help of language of thought. Language of thought is a distinct form of language which structures as well as processes thoughts. The linguistic features of thoughts are primarily syntactical. Cognitive states like belief, desire and intention are central to mental representation. Believing etc. is a relation between an organism and mental representation.

Syntactic properties and mechanism of belief change are defined as properties of mental representation. This is an organic function of neurophysiology. The neurophysiological function is the ultimate ground for the causal processes that are involved in information processing. The intentional feature of mental representation is through the object of experience that is definable. You connect the causal properties of a symbol with semantic properties, *via* its syntax. The reason of symbols is of higher order. The structure of syntax connecting the symbols acts as the language of thought.

Axiomatic derivation as above may yet give rise to a primordial question. How does motivation—intentionality arise? Let there be no confusion, can philosophers answer such a question as who was the father of Adam-Eve? Several revolutionary processes find their roots when a poet starts singing, 'deep in my heart I do believe!' With a .rational thinking there are no feelings as perceived by heart. The whole—entire organism with each and every cell of the body with their mitochondria continuously generating voluminous energy, a person has the motivation and intentionality arising not only from the whole brain but entire physiological processes in the body. Such an urge is a creative urge. It defies the elementary hierarchical model of motivation beginning from *Roti*, *Kapda*, *Makaan*—basic needs. It also gives a bypass to security and ego centric esteem needs. What a human being has created as a creative process would now be realized through self-actualization by himself.

Thus self actualization occurs with a quantum jump bypassing the model of hierarchy of needs. This creative process finds its expression in what was the basic substrate—attitude in the personality of the creative person. When scientists are thus possessed they invent Nobel Prize winning innovations. A literary genius writes 'Gitanjali' and Sri Aurobindo sings 'Savitri'.

Taking ontological metaphysics further to entirely abstract ideas, spirituality is experienced by most people and yet that may be considered as an attitude of personality. They are not physically identifiable and causally explainable. It has experiential quality that is understood by most.

Mahatma Gandhi would serve as most appropriate empirical evidence to understand metaphysics of spirituality. It is commonly asked, what was Mahatma Gandhi, was he an activist desiring social change, was he a freedom fighter fighting British imperialism, was he an environmentalist, was he a radical humanist follower of Ruskin that social change will prevail unto the last, was he a Hindu or was he a secular non-believer and so on. All such questions may be answered (w)holistically that he was a spiritual person. Spirituality is multidimensional. So that even Einstein—a discoverer of the fourth dimension—considered that future generations would scarce believe that such a human being did ever exist. Yet, spirituality is not only a high flown ideal of high flying people. It has the charismatic property that radically transforms everyone who comes in touch with them.

Psychologists will require a different mindset to study. The mind as a syntactic engine will not be aware of these mental features. Mind has no matter. Though brain transforms mental processes into thoughts, it does not have the capacity to transform mental representations that involve spiritual properties.

Taking the example of Mahatma Gandhi further, such a spiritual giant had the property so that an entire nation considers him '*Bapu,* Father of the Nation'. However, let it not be understood that every creative person should have this kind of powerful magnetic personality. There are diamonds with multiple carats. *Bapu* was that kind of a jewel of India that his creative spiritual process changed the course of several lives—generations. Yet, there may be a small diamond as well that may personify limited radiance of spirituality to a small circle of family, friends or society.

Those creative processes do involve brain functioning with semantics and syntactical connection which can best be surmised with a story.

Veda Vyas was assigned a task to leave entire wisdom to the posterity as a heritage for mankind. Vyas lays down that when he thinks, he cannot write. If a transcripter is provided, he must write as fast as he thinks!

Ganesha had such versatility. He lays down that he cannot pause when Vyas is thinking. The script now known as 'Purana' in eighteen volumes is written in Sanskrit. Each *shloka* has a format of four phases. The first three phases were intuitively derived as semantics. Easy flow that can be written fast. Fourth phase was so syntactically composed that Ganesha took a little longer to comprehend and write. Vyasa gained some time without a pause to think on the next *shloka*! We have arrived at a surmise that,

- Roger Sperry was a surgical genius who helped several thousand epilepsy patients. The research is now outdated by scientific advancement.
- Type A and Type B personalities are hypothetical. All normal human beings used both the hemispheres of their brain. Their professional skills may require the functions of one of the brains. This cannot be considered as absolute.
- Creative process involves diving deep into the entire being. Semantics thus derived would have to be formatted with a comprehensive syntax.
- Neurological processes that are thus involved in the creative process would need the functions of the whole brain.

We have comprehensively understood the process of intellectuation. Recapitulating Charak, we have narrated how the intellect functions. Yet, we have to understand another component of Pragnya. That is memory—Smruti. Intact memory is a prerequisite to intellectuation.

New knowledge is acquired by learning, for which an intact nervous system is a prerequisite. Whatever that is learnt afresh has to be retained as a short term memory or long term memory. Both of them involve proteins, however, they are different for both the types.

Recently acquired information is converted into long term memory through repetition, reinforcement with maybe acronyms (stubborn reinforcement occurs with embedding the memory with intense emotional content) recapitulation, revalidation that may modify the concept when stored as a long term memory. It is modified overtime with acquisition of new information by either further restructuring of the synaptic circuits or through non-use. Neurologically, the process is termed as neuronal plasticity.

It is important for understanding the underlying process as to how it constitutes a component of Pragnya. A person with loss of memory may be a patient of Parkinson's disease, Alzheimer's disease or may be just senile. We are concerned only with normal human beings. The proteins associated with memory loss are also identified and are likely to be available in therapeutic modes. We shall shun this discussion further.

Protein metabolism depends on expression of genes. Genetic map of each individual is inherited. This way it is likely that persons with a high retention of long term memory events may have inherited this trait of Pragnya.

Memory structure is primarily built around 5 senses, namely smell (olfactory nerve and centre), visual (optic nerve and orbital cortex), touch (sensory cortex in both hemispheres), hearing (8th cranial nerve and auditory centres in both hemispheres), taste (glossopharyngeal nerve to primary gustatory cortex). The lingual nerve is far more complex since this nerve also provides sensation as a branch of trigeminal nerve and derives some nerve fibres from other nerve structures as well. Yet, it is not concerned with the sensation of taste. Its relevance as a (w)holistic function with other centres of sense perception, we shall elucidate a little later.

Indian psychology, deriving inspiration from philosophical precepts, also postulates that additional information gathering apparatus is constituted by 28 *tanmatras.*

They are:

> Pruthvi, Api, Vayu, Tej, Akash, Shabd, Sparsha, Rupa, Rasa, Gandha, Prana, Paan, Vyaan, Udaan, Saman, Anamaya, Praanmaya, Manomaya, Vignyaanmaya, Anandmaya, Hands, Feet, Speech, Excretory organs, Reproductive organs Aatma, Antaratma, Parmatma.

The Rishi of Prashna Upanishads, Peeplod was approached by some pupils. They were anguished about some questions about the genesis and maintenance of the universe. The Rishi ordained them to discuss and contemplate between them for a year. When that was accomplished, Rishi told them that apart from ordinary senses, there are other organs in the body that probe the external environment and probing may extend to the whole universe. What obtains in the physical body that pertains even to the whole universe. Rishi Peeplod thus enumerated 28 tanmatras.

The pupils left the Ashram with satisfaction and the Rishi blessed each tanmatra and ordained them to function in tandem. He departed to the forest, trusting their autonomy with cooperation.

However, they started competing. Each one wanted to ascertain its own superiority. The eyes generated various panoramic vistas, speech and hearing produced several melodies and symphonies and hands not only painted, but also carved out beautiful statues. The excretory organs, namely anus was required to keep silent. Only sound that it can produce will be by farting. That is not good to hear. Every other organ ridiculed the organ of excretion.

Thus, slighted, excretory organs also decided to exercise its importance by dysfunction. Rather than functioning in tandem with other systems, its dysfunction produced flatulence. The abdomen started bloating up. Further on, the discomfort increased to such a level that all other sense organs had to plead, 'please, please regain your functionality again so that we again may function in orchestration.'

Functions of the hands and feet are well understood. With a little more elucidation we shall enlarge the importance of speech. A child at birth is both mute and may even not understand spoken speech. But, its auditory function would be normal. It starts understanding the voice of the mother. Mother tongue is the first heard sound by an infant. He gathers the impression of mother tongue in centres located in the brain. The process of memory storage of speech patterns will involve, in progressive order, centre for auditory nerve, situated in mid-brain. Here there is a complex interplay that exchanges information with other sensory centres such as sensation, exchange with synapses between trigeminal nerve, facial nerve, vagus nerve and even hypoglossal—essentially a motor nerve. The synapses are so dense that they generate a reticulum. Indeed the region is named as reticular formation. Its location extends from pons in the midbrain to way down in the medulla oblongata.

Above parable as well as complex synaptic interchanges both well illustrate that even in the lower parts of the brain, there is a synergistic collateral functioning (individual distinction between two hemispheres disappears, beginning at thalamus way down to medulla oblongata and spinal cord).

A person with his Pragnya, bright and stable, will thus automatically program his nervous system to function as a whole—(w)holistically.

Their relevance is important to generate a holistic concept of memory. However, their scientific investigation has been extensively studied for more than 150 years. A short scientific narration is further warranted to furnish empirical evidence for (w)holistic functioning.

Present understanding of memory mechanisms is derived from the studies, reflection and experimentation by neurosurgeons—Wilder Penfield and Karl Pribram, theoretical physicist David Bohm and Dennis Gabor, electrical engineer and physicist, and numerous psychologists including psychiatrists.

Wilder Penfield was the pioneer. As a neurosurgeon, he conducted experiments with galvanic current applied to the exposed brain. Significant conclusions emerged about memory storage and recall. They are:

1. The brain functions as a high fidelity recorder of the events of our lives. The most deterministic of which are those that have emotional content. The recordings are in time sequence. Their recall also occurs sequentially. When a person is paying conscious attention to any event, it is simultaneously recorded in the temporal lobe.
2. Feelings are experiential. Yet, their entire content is locked inextricably as a whole in memory.
3. There can be a simultaneous processing of two events such as, experiencing a present event and recalling the memory of remote past. They may or may not have any obvious relationship.
4. Penfield further reflects what psychologists would consider as subconscious and unconscious mind. What we have lived is recorded but all of that is not immediately available for recall. When access is established by whatever means (Freudian psychoanalysis or hypnotic regression to the past) one can relive in as vivid a form as when they happened.

Karl Pribram, another neurosurgeon, carried Penfield's research further. It was during his time that physicists developed not only theoretical concepts of a hologram but also produced a model of holographic image (this was instrumental in developing MRI, Positron Emission Tomography and other imaging techniques). Today, the concept is available to most of us, even in the form of a greeting card with a holographic image. To recapitulate, a hologram, even in a part, represents the complete whole.

Pribram established that memory is stored, not only in the memory centres, and within the axons emerging from them, but also as an electromagnetic field that surrounds them. It is also contained in non-functional dendrites around the cells.

Dendrites arise from the cell body and contribute in establishing communication with a large number of surrounding dendrites. However, they are not synaptically connected to each other. Pribram established, communication between dendrites occurs through an electrodynamic field.

Processing also occurs in webs of fine fiber branches of dendrites, as well as in the dynamic electrical fields surrounding the web of dendrites. The processing occurring around these dendritic trees can influence those trees of nearby neurons whose dendrites are entangled but not in direct contact.

This emerged as an empirical evidence by neuroscience that though brain areas are assigned to different functions region-wise, there is (w)holistic functioning between the cells of a particular region and adjacent regions as well. Research by Pribram is further buttressed with clinical evidence.

Cerebral stroke occurs when an artery gets blocked with an embolus or by a thrombus. When such an artery has no collateral circulation, the region of the brain supplied by the vessel dies. A major cerebral stroke clinically may produce paralysis of an extremity, or one half of the body that includes upper and lower limbs.

Clinical evidence suggests that the paralyzed limb or a lost function may be recovered. The recovery extends up to 18 months! This indicates that though dead cells cannot be made alive, dendritic webs can store functional memory and mutually communicate to each other through an electrodynamic field.

Creative expression of spirituality is a quantum jump to creativity. Its expression depends on how nature has ordained a personality.

Note

1. Chandrasekhar, S. (1990) [1987]. *Truth and Beauty. Aesthetics and Motivations in Science.* Chicago: The University of Chicago Press.

10
Epilogue

The authors make an attempt to arrive at a holistic understanding of Pragnya. It has involved and encompassed several disciplines ranging from philosophy, psychology and even physics.

Holism does not arise out of summation of its parts. Each part may represent the whole. Yet, a dissective discursive discussion is necessary to impart the precise meaning. When an attempt is made to speak or to write, it will have a beginning and its range may also be divided into parts in order to provide better understanding.

Finally, we disclose a hidden motive behind the presentation. Our prime aim was to arrive at a justification with tools obtained from Indian philosophy that a Pragnya quotient may arrive at. To justify psychology as a science, it must fulfill the primary criteria for being a science, viz. measurement. The process has begun with a hypothesis. This has undergone peer validation. Initial phase of application to a few hundred has also proved its validity as an instrument. Further applications may accrue when a wide range of psychologists, human resource managers, public administrators and policy makers will include this as one of the parameters for recruiting their best candidates.

At the end, we wish to give our short introduction. We have been primarily students of philosophy. So we end with a quote from the poet, Sir Edwin Arnold,[1]

"Measure not with words
Th'Immeasurable: nor sink the strings of thought
Into the Fathomless. Who asks doth err
Who answers, errs. Say nought!

The books teach Darkness was, at first of all,
And Brahm, sole meditating . . .

Veil after veil will lift—but there must be
Veil upon veil behind . . .

Pray Not! The Darkness will not brighten!
Ask Nought from the Silence, for it cannot speak!
Vex not your mournful minds with pious pains!
AH! Brothers, Sisters! Seek

Nought from the helpless gods by gift and hymn,
Nor bribe with blood, nor feed fruits and cakes;
Within yourselves deliverance must be sought;
Each man his prison makes . . ."

Note

1. Fragments of Ageless Wisdom—Sir Edwin Arnold, The Light of Asia.

Index